CLIENT ACQUISITION
blueprint

A **SIMPLE**, Step-By-Step Blueprint
For Creating an **EPIC** Marketing
Strategy & Online Presence

HUGO FERNANDEZ
CEO of Just DIgital Inc - A Top Rated Marketing Agency

ISBN-13: 978-1544042107
ISBN-10: 1544042108

Book Website: www.ClientAcquisitionBlueprint.com
Email: success@clientacquisitionblueprint.com

COVER DESIGN, BOOK INTERIOR
AND ILLUSTRATIONS BY LAURICE PLANDO
EDITING TEAM:
NEZA SKORC, ALEJANDRA SOLIS, EMILY OLSEN

Printed in the United States of America
First Revised Edition

Praise

"This book is a must-read for the entrepreneur that's serious about not only maximizing their brand awareness, but *building a world-class lifestyle.* **This book takes the headache and frustration out of marketing**, and gives you the exact blueprint to follow so you can grow your influence, customer experience, and most importantly your results to a whole new level."
-Peter Voogd, Founder of GameChangersMovement.com

"Just Digital delivers a ROI that is beyond 99.9% of their competition, because they understand that a great design isn't just one that "looks good" but one that directly increases sales of your product or service. Those who say, "You can't judge a book by its cover" forget that the cover is why you picked up the book in the first place. You must lead with your visual branding, so if you want to give your company the best chance of achieving extraordinary success in an already crowded marketplace, your first priority should be to hire Just Digital to separate YOU from the competition."
-Hal Elrod, author, The Miracle Morning (MiracleMorningBook. com)

"I sat with his team for a strategy session, where he taught me everything I needed to do to start crushing it on social media. He taught me both organic and paid advertising, and laid a complete and in depth strategy. Now I'm actually getting business from Facebook and Youtube!"
-Alex K, Top Producing Real Estate Agent

"Sets the bar in every respect"
-Zachary Weil, Executive Producer and Founder of Contact Light Films

"Provided me with more strategies than a 10 hour seminar from the so called gurus. Hugo is by far the best in the Marketing Space and business development."
-Rolando Castro "The Credit Coach", Credit Repair Solutions

"Hiring Hugo to do my brand development was one of the best business decisions I took this year! Those of you who know the design process understand that it can go in countless directions. Hugo manages what could be overwhelming potential with grace and a rare determination which results in the best possible option for each person's unique situation, personality, and goals. With him, you've got a brilliant eye as well as a real gift for communicating through various media speaking to you in the straightforward effective we all crave. Hugo and his team are highly skilled, sophisticated professional, and very easy to work with."
-Kevin Issa, CEO of Closeup Models Agency

"I personally worked with Hugo at Just Digital and I am always impressed by his commitment to helping my business grow. As a small business owner, it's difficult to always stay on target with respect to our marketing, sales, and end vision goals. Hugo has helped organize and keep us focussed on priorities so that we maintain efficiency and maximize our efforts. Most importantly, we are now working with clients who want to work with us (as opposed to chasing our clients) and that is priceless. Just Digital helped us not only understand that, but also paved the path for us to get there"
-Edward Pakdaman, Founder of Process Green

Dedication

To my wife, Mitra Silva, the most relentless entrepreneur and dreamer I've ever met. You inspire me to become more, to dream bigger, and stretch beyond what I think is possible. This book is published because you believed in me.

دوست دارم

To my mother and father, Juana and Alberto. You taught me to never quit. You gave me your everything though at times it felt like we had nothing. You taught me that money doesn't define your happiness nor your value, that you can always become more.

Los amo.

TABLE OF CONTENTS

BUILD AN EPIC BUSINESS

I believe entrepreneurs are wired to solve problems and if we help more entrepreneurs succeed, we can solve a lot of the problems in the world. Together we can design an epic future because *where others see problems, we see opportunities*. We don't settle for the way things are but instead, we work relentlessly to make them better.

I believe the role of a business is to create value and truly serve its customers. This is different than the old capitalistic mentality of a profit focused organizations. Those who continue to do a disservice to their customers by not putting them first, will struggle and lose market share in the coming decades. If you're creating value, you will create profit.

Why People Get Into Business

Most people, however, don't get started in business thinking, "How can I create value for others?" If you're like most business owners, you got into business for a mix of these three reasons:

1. **You love what you do**. If you're a florist, you love creating amazing bouquets. If you're a dentist, you love drilling teeth and helping people get a better smile.

2. **You want to live life on your terms and have more control**. You might have gotten tired of waiting for a vacation or asking to be let out of your job early so you can go to your kid's baseball practice. Maybe you thought your boss was an idiot and you could do things better. I quit my last "real job" because my boss wouldn't let me run a marketing campaign I wanted to run.

3. **You wanted a better quality of life.** You had the dream of being your own boss, taking time off whenever you wanted, and making millions of dollars with your business.

There's nothing wrong with any of these reasons. They're respectable and we all still want them. We start our business with these selfish reasons at first but quickly learn that the marketplace doesn't care about our selfish desires. It only cares about the value you create.

According to the Small Business Administration, there are around 28.2 million small businesses in the US. Unfortunately, 23 million of the small businesses make under $44,000 a year in gross sales. That's less than the national average household income of $55,000! Nobody got into business to struggle.

The Value Formula

So why are there so many businesses struggling? They violate *The Value Formula*.

The Value Formula is simply a framework I've used to understand and explain how business works. It's simple in nature, but powerful in effect. The role of a business should be to:

Create Value: This is through a product or service that people want. The more efficient you are at creating this value and the greater the value your product or service provides, the more money you'll make.

1. **Communicate that Value**: You need to be constantly communicating your value to the right people and lead them towards the decision of doing business with you. We'll cover how to do this in this book.

2. **Exchange that Value**: You need to be able to effectively exchange your value for money and deliver a world-class experience for your customers so they become raving fans.

A business is just a group of people working together towards a common goal, and as the leader of the organization, it's your job to ensure The Value Formula is being consistently applied. Don't ever neglect any of the three parts in the formula.

Over the past ten years, I've worked with hundreds of entrepreneurs making their ideas a reality, helping to better market their businesses, get more customers, and increase sales. I've worked with multi-million dollar businesses, high growth startups and many new ambitious entrepreneurs.

Time and time again, I've seen them violate or neglect one of these three areas. I've personally struggled with this in my business as well, but understanding the value formula allows you to figure out where you need to direct your attention.

Your ability to create value, communicate it, and exchange it will determine your success. In order to live out your dreams, you need to build and maintain the vehicle that honors the value formula. My mission with the Client Acquisition Blueprint is to help you establish the marketing foundation your business needs so you can build an epic business and live an epic life.

INTRODUCTION

If you've picked up this book, you know the importance and impact that a solid marketing plan can have on your business growth. Regardless of what you sell, whether it's a product or a service, if it's meant for children, adults, or the elderly, for the rich or not-so-rich; a complete online marketing strategy is fundamental to your success.

However, with an overwhelming amount of information and resources out there, knowing where to start can be a daunting task and most business owners simply neglect putting any marketing plan in place. They rely on unpredictable marketing methods, struggle with inconsistent cash flow, and never put a system in place for predictable growth.

The truth is, most business owners have no clue how to market and grow their business. They're lawyers, accountants, doctors, and dentists. They're writers, chefs, florists, and mechanics. They're some of the most passionate people I've ever met. They love their craft but tend to shy away from all this "marketing stuff."

Why This Book Exists

More and more people have decided to take control of their financial future and live life on their terms by starting their own business. The old model of "go to school, get good grades, get a good job and work it for 40 years then retire at 60," is simply no longer working for people.

So they decide to ditch the 9-5 day and chase their dreams, only to find themselves in a 95 hour work week and still struggling to make ends meet. It saddens me to see the 60 year old business owner with no retirement and still struggling with unpredictable cash flow in the business after 25 years.

If you're in business and are struggling, you're not alone, but it's time to change that. But hoping clients will just show up at your office is a guaranteed way to continue stressing yourself out. By putting into practice some simple marketing strategies and consistently taking actions to promote your business, you can join the top 20% of businesses that are thriving.

Who This Book Is For

This book is meant for the common person who has a dream and decided to follow it through building a business. This isn't a marketing textbook, it's a practical guide for the busy business owner or startup founder. If you work for a business and are responsible for marketing it, it's your responsibility to help the business succeed.

If you're a successful business owner, you might find new strategies or ideas that can continue to accelerate your success. Share this book with your team, and with other business owners who you connect with.

If you're a seasoned marketer, you have a specialized skill that can dramatically affect the success and finances of business owners. I've seen it change their lives forever and I believe it's our duty to help them succeed.

This book is not aiming at becoming the next "Online Marketing Bible". It's simply what I've learned through my life's journey of helping others grow their businesses.

I became an entrepreneur by default, hustling since I was 3 when I would grab customers by the hand and take them to my mom's food stand in Mexico. It was a way to survive and it was our shot at having something more.

Over the past five years as CEO of Just Digital Inc., a top digital marketing agency based in Los Angeles, I've had the privilege of implementing these basic strategies across multiple industries. We've worked with hundreds of entrepreneurs making their ideas a reality, helping to better market their businesses, get more customers, and increase sales.

The main goal of this book is to simplify the most common and proven concepts and techniques so even those with little to no marketing knowledge and experience can build an online presence that will help them grow their business. It's written with the small business owner in mind who, more often than not, struggles to predictably increase sales. Reading this book and following these simple steps might just be what your business needs from you.

What Is "The Client Acquisition Blueprint"?

In this book, we'll help you create a blueprint that will outline all of the online promotional, advertising and communication activities related to your business, as well as go through the strategies, tools and tactics to help you skyrocket your growth.

From strategy to execution, we'll cover the ten essential keys to an epic marketing strategy and growth plan. When thinking of marketing, there are three fundamental blocks or categories we can place things into:

These three fundamental blocks are broken down into a framework I created, laid out in the next ten chapters. Throughout the book, you'll discover:

THE 3 BUILDING BLOCKS OF MARKETING

1. Unshakeable Foundation
2. Converting Leads to Clients
3. Getting Massive Attention

---

1. A simple marketing strategy you can swipe and deploy in your business.

2. The Ten Keys to an EPIC Online Presence.

3. How to get massive attention using organic and paid strategies: The secret missing piece that can get you off the cash flow rollercoaster and allow you to scale your growth.

4. Advertising Basics: How to launch your first Google Adwords and Facebook Advertising campaign and how to maximize your daily ad budget.

5. The Profit Path: How will you make money and how do you know if what you're doing is actually working?

6. How to create irresistible offers, lead magnets, and landing pages to convert website visitors into leads.

7. Marketing Automation: The backbone of a scalable business.

8. How to structure your first automated follow up sequence so you never forget to follow up with unconverted leads.

Clients Or Customers?

Throughout the book I alternate between the term *client* and *customer*. I mean the same thing: someone who exchanges money for your value (your product or service). I chose the title "The Client Acquisition Blueprint" simply because professional service firms call their patrons, *clients*. We provide a professional service and refer to the people we serve as clients. A lot of the examples are from past clients we've served and they refer to their patrons as clients as well.

There's a rather silly semantic debate that argues you should have clients and not customers, claiming that clients are somehow worth more or should be treated better than customers. There's more prestige and care that goes into a client than a customer, they claim.

I say that's a pointless discussion. Someone that transacts with you and your business, regardless of the dollar amount, should warrant the same effort. They exchanged their hard earned dollars for your promise of value, so over-deliver and you'll have a client for life and a raving fan that promotes your business to everyone they know.

How To Use
The Client Acquisition Blueprint

Marketing is a game of patterns, and once you find patterns that work, stick to them to drive growth for your business but keep things flexible and continue to test new strategies. Never stop marketing!

The biggest mistake I see business owners make when they start getting success in marketing is that they simply stop. They get busy or overwhelmed and take their foot off the gas. When they want to start things back up, they've lost all momentum.

Test everything.
Having a plan for your marketing activities doesn't mean that once it's laid out, it's all said and done. It's important to test everything. Test your assumptions, test your campaigns, test everything. It's ok to assume things (about your business, your value proposition, your clients) but never hold these things as absolute truths unless you've tested them over and over again.

Innovate and adapt.
An online marketing plan should eventually change to adapt to the reality of your business, the value you offer, the channels available, and the clients you're serving at the moment.

Things change rapidly in this new economy and my mission in this book is to give you the true and tested fundamentals of a solid marketing strategy.

Don't spend excessive time on channels that are not frequented by your target audience simply because the channel is available. Just because a guru told you to be on every social media channel doesn't mean you should waste your time on Snapchat if it's not working for you. It makes no sense and it's not very efficient to spend your time and limited resources trying to communicate with people who don't value you or that aren't your Perfect Client Profile.

Your Client Acquisition Blueprint should adapt to the shifts in the market and new trends. Case in point, all the companies that were using Vine will now have to adapt their marketing plans to refocus those resources elsewhere. But having a solid foundation allows you to keep improving regardless of the marketing channel shifts.

You might wonder—why even prepare a plan if you'll be changing it sooner or later? The reason is quite simple. Having it written makes it real. It serves as a reminder of everything you and your team agreed to do, how you'll do it and by when. There is a clear silver lining to it, making it easy to refocus when you get distracted by all the noise. It ensures you reach your business goals, and it makes it easier to review the results of your marketing efforts.

The truth is most organizations are strapped for resources. Knowing what to do with these resources is crucial. Whether that's financial resources or pure startup hustle, energy and effort, having a blueprint to follow will help you maximize those resources and stay consistently marketing your value to potential clients.

AN UNSHAKEABLE FOUNDATION

Everything needs a foundation. A house without solid foundation will collapse in cases of any natural catastrophes, as will your business if you don't take the time to work on its own version of solid foundation. To do so, there's no better place to start than with a solid strategy, then continue with your brand (Chapter 2), website (Chapter 3), online accounts and profiles (Chapter 4) and social media (Chapter 5).

Your Epic Growth Strategy

"Strategy without tactics is the slowest route to victory. Tactics without strategy is the noise before defeat." -Sun Tzu

The word "strategy" often makes small business owners or those in charge of marketing in a small company wonder, "What exactly is there to strategize about? Let's go!"

This is a word that is often reserved for executives of impressive companies. Companies that operate with huge budgets and employ hundreds, if not thousands, of people.

Having a strategy, however, is not a luxury or something that is exclusive to these companies. Every time there's a plan, there should be a strategy that precedes it—why should your company carry out this plan in the first place? What does the plan aim to achieve, how and by when? It can be as simple as a single phrase or a short paragraph, one that summarizes the end goal all the planned efforts will be aiming to reach.

The strategy should be clear and simple enough for everybody to understand what you're aiming at, even if they don't read the rest of your marketing plan. This is by far the most important action, as it is the foundation for everything to come.

The one thing your strategy should always begin with is a simple statement of three things.

> ### STRATEGY: 3 SIMPLE STATEMENTS
>
> 1. Who you are as a business, Why you're in a business, What you believe
> 2. Who your Perfect Clients are
> 3. What value you provide your clients

This might sound simple, but it usually turns out to be trickier than expected. We'll cover the "who you are" question in the Branding chapter. In this chapter we'll explore "who your customers are" and "what value you provide."

It's important to have these elements clearly laid out because chances are you'll be collaborating with more people when developing your marketing. Your internal team, your employees that service your customers, your web designer, videographer, etc—they'll all ask these questions. It's important to have them written down so that your answers don't shift with every conversation you have, resulting in non-consistent marketing material and campaigns.

Stop Trying To Be Different!

When trying to figure out their value proposition, people tend to ask, "Well, what makes us different than every other person doing the same thing?" They make the mistake of focusing on their competition, rather than on their customers. Your main goal should be to provide more value to the people you serve, not merely be different for the sake of standing out in the marketplace.

Developing a Unique Selling Proposition or Value Proposition based on your competition will most likely be irrelevant to the customers you're trying to attract. And, at the end of the day, your main goal should not be to be different, but to speak to your customers' needs better than anybody else, thus creating more value for them to address their fundamental needs.

Most companies, instead of thinking about their customers' needs and the unique solution they provide those customers, look at the competition and how they're doing things, and then try to figure out a way to be different. Which is definitely not the way to go, since your competition won't be the one consuming your products or services.

The other problem with the 'being different' approach is that most business owners are afraid to push the envelope and be truly different. As humans, we'd much rather conform to the status quo than be seen as outsiders. More often than not, people tend to create "me too" marketing. We're much better at mirroring or copying others than we are at thinking different.

So the end result is: marketing that is only slightly different, different but not valuable, or worse, you actually look and sound like everyone else.

The Long Term, Sustainable Approach To The Value Proposition

Everything we create for clients is based on real value—the value you've already created in your business. If we can't find something in your existing business, then we go to the drawing board and always find ways to improve the value creation process. We define value as something useful, something that improves the quality of life for your clients, improves the transaction, and fundamentally solves the problem or fulfills the desire of your clients.

The best place to find out what value you truly provide is to simply ask:

> ▷ **Ask your past customers.** What was your biggest challenge/ frustration/problem with [whatever you helped them with]. How did it feel once that problem was gone?

▷ **Ask potential customers.** Big companies spend millions on market research. You don't have to. I've asked strangers at Starbucks and people in my office building.

▷ **Go read bad reviews or comments people have about your industry.** You'll find gold here and lots of missed opportunities.

This is not a one time process either. It's engaging and truly listening to your clients on an ongoing basis. It's not some boring survey they fill out after the transaction. It's you and your people truly caring about your customers at every transaction. It's asking them questions about their life, their problems, their dreams and desires.

Write down a list of questions you'd like to ask your clients. Have it handy. Ask them at every opportunity.

Not only will you fine tune your value proposition, you'll find marketing gold there as well. Almost every time we ask our clients at Just Digital these questions, we find their answers to not even be about the service we provide, but their raw human emotions. They're happy we take the frustration and complication out of the marketing process. They say the value we provide is that we "listen to them," they feel like we truly care about their business, and we explain things to them well. Though we do awesome work for them that gets incredible results, there's seldom very much about that.

The next step is to express it in a simple sentence. I like to think of it as a tweet, if it's longer than that, your value proposition is too complicated. The way you express it is simple:

Who Allows You To Do Your Best Work?

Once you define the identity of your company (in Chapter 2) and your unique selling proposition, based on your potential customers' wants and needs, you'll also, many times without even

---

THE VALUE PROPOSITION FORMULA

We help [*Perfect Client Profile*]
with [*the real value you will provide*].

---

realizing it, define your Perfect Client Profile. This is basically the ideal client you'd like to serve and attract.

By having a clear idea about you and your company, you'll get much closer to the concept of your perfect client. Why?

Because who you are is who you attract. So, it's essential that you know yourself and your company well, and be intentional about it.

As a result, your values attract people with similar values, and your beliefs, goals, and mission will be reflected in your customers' beliefs, goals, and mission. These are the customers that will let you do your absolute best work.

For example, a video production company in Hollywood came to Just Digital for some help. As most new companies in a competitive environment, they took on whatever work came their way. As a nimble video crew, they could produce just about anything, and they were. From local business videos to short comedies, they were doing it all for the first few years. But the Founder and Executive Producer, despite loving comedy himself, wasn't quite sure about the direction he had chosen (or lack thereof).

During the strategy sessions we had, he continually mentioned his passion for social causes, how storytelling catalyzed change, and how much he enjoyed working with a nonprofit in particular. It was brought up in the conversation over and over again, which led to the logical question of why not focus on nonprofits? In the end, the owner rebranded the company suitable to the new target market, with a clear focus on nonprofit organizations.

He was able to attract talent that aligned with that mission and attract better paid productions. The owner is more fulfilled and engaged than ever, the company is impact oriented, mission driven, and producing their best work ever. After three years of focusing on nonprofits, he's going through another change in his strategy, but the work we did in the beginning still serves as the foundation for the next phase of growth.

Your Perfect Client Profile

Just because someone liked you and paid you money doesn't mean they're your ideal client. We've all had crappy clients, you know, the clients that make us cringe every time they call us. Clients that don't appreciate your work or that simply don't get it. The goal of the Perfect Client Profile is to eliminate or reduce the number of bad clients, while exponentially increasing the number of good clients that allow you to do your best work.

We use two methods to start zeroing in on who your Perfect Client is.

1. If you have less than a few hundred clients
Make a list of all your clients, then grade them A, B and C. A is the most enjoyable and easy to work with and turns the highest profit. They value your work, leave you awesome reviews and tell their friends and colleagues about you. All your clients evaluate your performance anyway, now it's your turn to evaluate whether they're a good fit for you or not

2. If you have more than a few hundred clients
Try to create a few categories of customers and do the same thing. For example, you might have a wholesale and retail side of your business. On the wholesale side you might serve five different types of businesses. On the retail, you might see 2-3 types of people walk into your store.

Shortcut:
A faster and simpler way to do this is to simply think of your favorite client. The client or customer that makes you happy to see

them. When they call, you smile. They rave about you, they bring you more business, and they seldom complain.

Once you have this done, then it's time to trim the fat and start building an intentional business.

1. **Cut out the C clients.** They'll free up space and energy for bigger and better things. Don't be afraid of revenue losses here. You'll make them back 10x with your Perfect Clients

2. **Find ways to bump the B clients to A** or cut them off.

3. **Figure out how to get more of the A clients** and seek to understand them better.

You may find that you don't actually enjoy working with a lot of your existing customer base and it may lead you to rethink and overhaul your business. Great. Otherwise, your business will eventually fail.

Or you might find that you're pretty happy with the people you're serving and you might just add another market segment. A friend of mine owns an event venue and he also hosts his own nightlife events with different musical performances. He's constantly evaluating which nights perform best, which side of his business produces the most revenue and which one he enjoys the most. He found out that doing corporate events were the most profitable (around $20,000 per event and very little headache) so he created a marketing campaign to attract more of those types of clients. But he has a passion for culture and music, so he still keeps that side of the business running profitably.

Once you've got this down, it's time to get specific with your Perfect Client Profile. Pick a specific person in your A list and ask yourself these broader questions first:

1. **How did I get this A client?**
   a. Can I get more the same way? Chances are you're not maximizing that marketing channel.

2. **Where do their friends hang out?**
   a.   Do they buy similar products/services?
   b.   How can I get around more of these A clients?

Then you can get down to the basic and specific details of that Perfect Client. Where they live, what their life is like and how they think. Some marketers call this your customer avatar, buyer persona, or broadly known as your target market. Regardless, they all do the same thing: list out your ideal customer's qualities. The more detailed you are with these, the easier it will be to identify where they are and how you can attract them to your business.

Here's a starting point for you: start with the basics, then get deeper into the ones that make sense for your business. Personally, I go as deep as possible. Just don't break any laws or turn people off.

Some questions you can ask directly ("where did you go to school?") and others you have to just observe, listen, or infer from other things they may tell you.

Some data you might not know how to use just yet, but there might be dots you can connect in the future. It'll be insight that your competition won't have because they simply never asked their clients. Remember, as humans, we tend to follow patterns and habits. Each of these questions gives you insight into how your customers behave and what motivates them:

▷   Age + Gender

▷   Marital Status: For how long? Where did they meet?

▷   Education: Where they went to school and what they studied

▷   What they do for work: For how long? How often do they switch jobs? Have they switched careers?

▷   Location: Homeowner, renter etc? Do they move often or stay in one place? Do they like their current location?

▷   Family Size

▷ Income

▷ Interests: This one you can have a lot of fun with. What brands do they own? What car do they drive? Why? What do they do for fun? Do they eat at home or eat out? What's their favorite restaurant?

▷ How do they make decisions? As a couple? Do they ask friends, do research to gather all the facts, or trust their instinct?

▷ Charitable contributions

▷ Do they travel? Where's the last place they traveled to?

▷ Who do they listen to for information and news?

There are endless questions you can ask and you may wonder: why do some of these matter? They matter to your ideal customers. There's a lot already influencing them so you want to know what those things are. Plus you can also get a more rounded picture of their life. A couple of examples:

"Do they eat at home or eat out?" This may tell you if they're busy and always on the move, and the restaurants they visit might give you an indication of income level, as well as the car they drive.

▷ If you know their profession, you can simply Google their [profession] plus the word salary to get a rough estimate of income.

Of course, some things you can infer pretty safely, others you can't and you have to test your assumptions. The goal is to know them better than they might know themselves. In order to influence someone, you need to know what already influences them.

Bridging Gaps. Designing Possibilities.

However, this doesn't mean that these things define them or that you should just assume that your customers react to things like you would. You should still take the time to get to know and understand them, to put yourself in their position and get a good grasp on what they find important and what has an impact and influence on their lives. By doing so, you'll be able to create a bridge between what you offer and care about and the issues and needs of your customers.

When I explain marketing and business to people, I often use a concept I so creatively coined "The Bridge." It's basically a much more human and value driven framework to explain how marketing comes together with everything else. By building this bridge between your customers and your company, you'll be able to offer them a way to get from their side, where their needs and desires exist and they can't seem to address in a satisfying manner, to your side, where you can give them access to your unique solutions for their issues and the value your company can provide them. Before we proceed with The Bridge, let's take a moment to actually define two key terms that are commonly misused and abused in the business world.

The Real Definition of Marketing

Marketing is the communication of value to the people you want to serve in an effort to lead them to a decision of doing business with you.

The real definition of sales: *Sales is an exchange of value.* Simple as that. You have a product or service that is valuable to your customers, they give you money, you deliver that value.

The more efficient you get at communicating and exchanging that value, the more money you'll make. Make it easy for people to understand your value, then make it easy for people to exchange and receive that value.

Delivering value to the people you serve is what will help your company thrive in the long run, and the bridge is essential in this process—it is what will enable you to communicate the value of your product or service to your potential customers and convince them to cross the bridge with you, to take the journey with you, to accept your

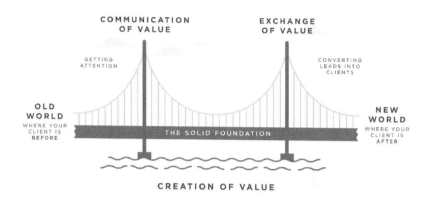

"price of admission," which can be something as simple as attention and trust, and as a result, improve the quality of their lives.

Your marketing strategy is the foundation of The Bridge, holding it together and making sure it doesn't collapse. You also have your sales process, which, despite it needing to work with marketing, is a process on its own and should be treated as such. So, through the marketing process, you'll let your customers know about the value your product or service can bring into their lives and your sales process is what will convince them to exchange their money for this value.

This approach helps humanize marketing, especially comparing it to the way marketing was done up until not too long ago: we're talking about when the most common terms discussed were funnels and people in terms of datasets, giving you money if and when prospects made it through your company's marketing funnel.

The Profit Path: Part One

Once you have your company's identity thought out, you know what type of customers you'd like to attract, you understand their needs, you have your value clearly set up and your Bridge is built with a strong marketing and sales process, it's time to get to the important part: how will you actually make more money?

What you need is to define your Profit Path. This might sound really complicated, and most likely what popped up in your head was complex multi-tab Excel sheets that nobody understands and have formulas and scripts that go on for days. Yes, you can do that, but it's actually anything but complex. It's just basic math and setting targets that you'll actually stick to.

How I Almost Bought A Hummer When I Was 10 Years Old

I became an entrepreneur by default, hustling since I was 3 when I would grab customers by the hand coming out of the local church and take them to my mom's food stand in Mexico. It was a way to survive and it was our shot at having something more. Looking back, this taught me the basics of business and money.

One particular summer though, at age 10, my mom made Mexican food to sell at construction sites around the Seattle area. I would spend my days watching my sisters while she was away and running my little Mexican candy business.

One day, as I was taking inventory of my candy and watching TV, a Hummer advertisement came on. Remember those big yellow gas guzzling SUVs? As a 10 year old, I thought it was the coolest thing in the world!

It looked unstoppable, a beast running over the mountains, and I stopped counting my candy and focused entirely on the ad. At the end of the commercial, there was the price —$50,000—which was around two years of income for my family.

But for a 10 year old, $50,000 was just a number, and I sat in our living room for the rest of the afternoon figuring out how many pieces of candy I needed to sell to have enough money to buy a Hummer. Once I figured out my plan, I ran to my mom and told her about it.

She laughed.

The goal was insane, especially because my family couldn't even afford to buy me a bicycle nor a full happy meal at McDonalds for all of us. Even if bought the Hummer, I obviously couldn't drive it. But I didn't care. I could wait five years until I got my driving permit. I was determined to hustle and make it happen. So my mom decided to help me out and she made some extra snacks for me to sell. I was going to buy that Hummer.

That summer was my most profitable summer ever, and even though I only missed my goal by $49,000, it was a blast trying to reach it. I was able to buy a kitchenette for my sisters to play with and a bike for myself. We lived in a pretty rough neighborhood though, so my bike was stolen in five days flat. I don't think I've ever owned a bike since, nor do I want a Hummer anymore.

The story may seem trivial, but it highlights an important point for any business owner. I've personally repeated this same process every year since (and I've gotten better at hitting my sales goals). As a kid, and even now, it wasn't really about the money or the Hummer, it was about something cool I wanted, a crazy dream, and having the vehicle for achieving it (my business).

Figuring out this sales and marketing stuff has the power to change your life. But you need to set clear targets and do the math.

Do The Math + Set Clear Targets

This is the same approach I've used for multimillion dollar companies. Yes, it's that simple, yet I'm amazed at how few business owners actually take the time to set concrete goals and sales quotas. From doctors to accountants, from mechanic shops to flower shops, the common request is, "I want more clients!" Then I ask, "How many more?" The answer is more often than not, "As many as I can get."

Tony Robbins says when we ask for stuff, we're not specific enough. A lot of us say, "I want more money," and life says, "Here's $1, shut up and get out of here." As leaders of our companies, we need to set clear targets. If you don't know the target, how will your team know? Work for any sales organization or team and you'll see they track these on a daily basis.

The first step to actually acquiring customers is to figure out the basic growth metrics and targets. Figure out:

What are you selling?

What products or services are the most profitable for your business? What's the quickest way to the cash? If you're trying to kickstart sales or turnaround a business, this is a perfect place to start. Your business may offer 60 different products or services, but only 20% of them account for 80% of the revenue. Take inventory, find the winners, cut the extra weight. When Steve Jobs returned to Apple in 1997 amidst declining sales, his team was unable to explain why they had so many different products. Unable to find a good answer, he cut 70% of the products and went to work on the core products that eventually made Apple great. It cleared the way for the iPod, iTunes, the iPhone and the iPad.

How much are you selling it for?

There's always someone who will be willing to sell your product or service for less. Don't play that game if you're a small business. There's no inherent value in being cheap. Instead, figure out how to provide more value for your clients. One of the fastest ways to make more money is to simply charge more. Most business owners are simply afraid to really charge what they're worth because they don't want to turn away clients.

How many sales do you want?

Set monthly, quarterly and yearly goals. Then we can start figuring out a marketing plan for making sure we attract enough leads and prospects to your business.

Once you have that part of the Profit Path done, then you can start gathering more data and tracking the key metrics on a weekly and monthly basis:

1. The number of leads your business gets.

2. The number of total sales:
   a. Number of transactions
   b. Average transaction price

3. Your sales conversions: Out of every ten people you talk to, how many actually become clients?

4. Average customer value: How much does a customer, on average, spend on your products or services in a year?

The easiest way is to define the desired revenue and input the average transaction price to see how many sales you need to reach your goal.

For example, if a plastic surgeon would like to reach a $1,000,000 yearly gross revenue, and his average procedure is $3,000, he'll need 334 patients to reach his goal. This can be the same for a cosmetic dentist. Pretty simple, but you'll be surprised how many people don't set simple goals like this. As their marketing partner, our job would be to identify the top most profitable procedures he does and that he actually enjoys, then focus on marketing those. If his average procedures get raised or we're marketing higher priced procedures, and we factor in the one year follow ups to get a total of $10,000 patient value, then we only need 100 patients to reach the goal. This also allows us to figure out the maximum price we're willing to pay in marketing to acquire one patient.

If his sales conversions rate is 10%, then he needs 1000 leads to get these 100 patients. Is this doable? Is his sales process in place? Is his staff properly trained to handle the volume of inquiries? How can we increase the conversion rate to 15% or 20%?

Actually seeing the numbers on a regular basis will give you the clarity you need to rethink your approach. You'll be able to decide if you need more clients, have your existing clients buy more often, or increase the prices and have your existing clients pay more for your products or services. There is, of course, a fourth option as well, and it is to make a combination of all three that suits your business perfectly.

How To Budget For Marketing

There's an important point to mention when talking about the Profit Path and Strategy in general. Once you know your desired numbers, then you can start budgeting for marketing.

Most of the activities mentioned in the following nine chapters require some investment. Some are cheaper than others, but they're never free. They all require either an investment of money, time, or both.

The usual recommendation is to take your top line revenue and then put 10-20% of it aside for marketing purposes. This number can and should adjust as your business scales and your growth plans change. It also varies by industry, your individual profit margins, and your market conditions. You might find that it makes more sense to be at 5-10% and still achieve the growth goals you have.

Taking the 10- 20% range, if you're a $500,000 business (or want to have a $500,000 business) then you're looking at spending $50,000 to $100,000 in marketing. Most of our clients find this to be a reasonable number when all things are factored in.

A simple way to divide your budget in this scenario is:

1. **50% to pay for your team (time):** either your internal marketing team or agency partner. $50,000 might get you an entry level or mid level marketer depending on your market and location.

2. **50% of that can be allocated to paid advertising** (discussed in more detail in Chapter 10). You might also include software and other marketing expenses in either of these categories.

Again, as your business scales, the ratios and budget will most likely shift but the framework will remain the same. In the $500k business example, you could potentially afford expert help, but you may choose to rely on just word of mouth, referral and grassroots marketing. This might include you spending time on social media or networking with people who can refer you business. Your first year while you build, you might even create your own website and marketing material.

But having this amount set aside will help you estimate what you can and cannot spend on. It'll tell you what options you have available. It will keep you in check and also help you better calculate your Return on Investment, as well as control your efforts and find ways to optimize every dollar you spend on marketing. Despite this sounding quite intimidating at the beginning, without marketing, your stream of potential clients will never get to its full potential, and you'll be on a constant cashflow rollercoaster.

The Value Ladder: Create Massive Value For Your Clients And Predictable Cash Flow

This is one of my favorite concepts to share with people and it has revolutionized the way our clients sell. This is a concept that Russell Brunson introduced in his book DotCom Secrets, and its purpose is to create a ladder of increasing value that your customers can "ascend." The goal is to create a higher lifetime value for each client and to keep providing value at every level.

The value ladder goes beyond just having a customer and offering them a single product or service. It focuses on how to create more value for the customer, and by providing them more value, getting more revenue in return. The higher your clients ascend, the higher the price also gets.

It's directly linked to increasing the sales income, but instead of looking outside and trying to find new customers (the logical first reaction and/or idea for a company), it looks inside to the existing customers and poses the question of how to convince them to agree to a higher exchange—*more value for more money.*

THE VALUE LADDER

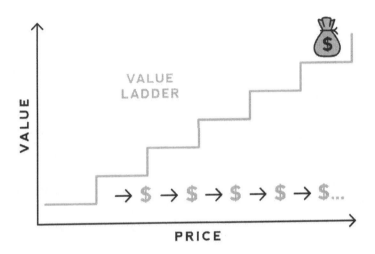

It's the basic concept of the natural progression of the customers to ascend to the maximum value that you can deliver.

A question I often use to challenge our clients to think bigger is: "If somebody came to your office today and offered your company a million dollars, what would they get in return?" It forces you to think about creating more value for your clients. It may also scare some people just thinking about it, but the fact is you have to be ready for the opportunities.

After I complained that our clients were maxing out at our highest price point, my business coach bluntly pointed out, "You have nothing more expensive to sell them!" Again, seems obvious, but often our clients want more of us, they want more value, and they're willing to pay for it. We just have to create the value and offer it.

It doesn't matter if you already have customers at that level or not, but it's important to understand how high you can go because it will open a window of opportunities for defining more steps of your ladder, steps which will be easier for you to sell to your existing customers.

For example, a dentist would start building the value of the customer by offering different services, such as normal check-ups, then whitening, then retainers, and so on, each higher in value than the previous one, until the absolute maximum is reached, while still offering the ongoing services such as regular checkups every three months.

Key Distinctions In Marketing Strategy, Campaign, Channel, and Media Type

To wrap up this chapter, there's a few key distinctions we like to make as you keep reading. These are important to note so you can create a complete and well rounded marketing strategy and not get overwhelmed with where things fit into the process.

Strategy
The overall direction, focus, and plan. Example: Double sales in 12 months by selling your most profitable product to your new Perfect Client Profile. Your strategy should align with who you are as a company and who you want to attract into your business so that you're able to deliver your best work.

Campaign
Orchestrated promotion or activities aimed at achieving a specific goal. Example: Drive more ecommerce sales by offering a sweepstakes giveaway or launching a new product, or targeting a specific demographic for a period of time on a specific channel. There's usually a start and end to these.

Channel
In the old economy you have TV, radio, print (newspapers, Yellow Pages, outdoor media such as billboards, buses, benches).

In the new economy you have social media (Instagram, Facebook, Twitter, etc), paid online advertising (Google Adwords, Facebook Ads, etc), your website, blogging/ authority sites. We'll cover these channels in upcoming chapters. I also sometimes refer to these as platforms or networks.

Media Type

This is the actual type of content you'll be putting and marketing on each channel. With TV you obviously run a video ad, now you'd run that on Youtube or Facebook. On Instagram you'd post photos and videos. Your strategy and campaign would dictate what channels you're posting on, how often, for what reasons and goals, and to what audience. Online you're able to track an incredible amount of data on your media type and channels, from views, engagement, and conversions.

Thinking of marketing in this layered format—having clear targets, and getting your strategic foundation set—we can then move on to creating your Client Acquisition Blueprint and start actually building the stuff that will bring you more qualified leads, prospects and ultimately more sales.

Designing An Instantly Recognizable Brand

CHAPTER 2

"A brand is how your clients feel about you, it's about how they think of you and how they identify you. An authentic brand is the only thing your competition can't replace." –Hugo Fernandez

Your brand is one of the first things people see. It's the perception people have of your business. It's an indicator of quality and value, and you must be intentional about designing the brand you want because if you don't, you're leaving it to others to decide. However, a brand is much more than design and visual elements, it's how you make your prospects feel, what emotions they attach to your products or services, and it's about the beliefs and values your company embodies.

When it comes to designing an authentic brand, there are three key components that serve as the foundation to your brand. With the proper brand strategy, you can literally choose where you want to be positioned in the marketplace.

You And Your Company

The beginning of a brand is its identity and that starts with you. What do you stand for? What are your values and beliefs? What's your purpose, why do you believe your company exists? What's your mission? Most entrepreneurs never develop that level of self-awareness, and most struggle to develop a powerful brand. It's essential to know who you are as an individual and as a leader of your organization, so that you can attract the right kind of people into your business. From your employees, your vendors, and ultimately your customers, they need to understand who you are on a much deeper psychological level, and be able to relate parts of their own personal identity to that of your business.

Your Audience And Customers

You need to know their struggles and their pain, their dreams and their desires. We did some of this work in the strategy section, and these are the people on the other side of The Bridge. Looking at the brands they already consume is an easy way to create a brand that attracts them.

The Visual Elements Of Your Brand

This refers to everything visual that represents your brand, from your logo, website, colors, font choices, physical marketing material (stationery, brochures, signage, etc), to your office interior design and layout. Based on these elements, your prospects will start to consciously or subconsciously make decisions, prior to even engaging with you. You could also think of these elements as your brand's wardrobe. People will judge you based on how you look, whether you like it or not. These visual elements are what we'll focus on in this chapter, but first, let's dive into how the right branding strategy allows you to completely dominate your market and build a global empire.

How Your Brand Can Be Fluid And Skyrocket Your Profits

Once you fully understand these three key elements of an authentic brand, you can adapt to your audience depending on what you're trying to achieve. I love studying corporate brand strategy because it highlights this point.

Car companies do this brilliantly. Take for instance the Volkswagen Group. They own the Volkswagen brand of cars, but they also own Porsche, Audi, Bentley, Bugatti, Rolls Royce, and Lamborghini. But there's an obvious twist to it all: the effort put into selling a Volkswagen Jetta is very different from that behind selling a Bugatti.

Toyota's luxury brand is Lexus, and until 2016 they had a brand, Scion, that was almost exclusively made to attract younger customers.

Luxottica is a company many people have never heard of, yet it's the world's largest eyewear company. They design, manufacture, and distribute products through their own retail channels: LensCrafters, Sunglass Hut, Apex by Sunglass Hut, Pearle Vision, Sears Optical, Target Optical, and Glasses.com to name a few. They own notable brands like Ray-Ban and Oakley, and they manufacture frames for Chanel, Prada, Giorgio Armani, Burberry, Versace, Dolce and Gabbana, Coach, and many more.

You could also look at almost any product (food, entertainment, etc) and reverse engineer their strategy by searching for who owns them. You'll find an elaborate brand and marketing strategy aimed at one thing: *sell more of the same stuff to different people.* It's almost scary when you start digging because you'll notice that only a handful of companies actually create or control almost everything in the market.

The point here is simply to illustrate the power branding can have, and to get you to think bigger when you're creating your foundation. There's obviously more to this strategy and running a multinational empire than just branding, but it's a combination of the three key elements of brand building, and seeing how they relate to each other, that can open doors to places and successes you couldn't imagine in your wildest dreams.

The first thing that cannot be stressed enough is that *consistency is key.* Understanding what your brand represents and communicating it consistently will help the customers remember your business and connect with it on a subconscious level. In today's visual world, these elements are much more important than they ever were, and the quality of the materials is a strong indicator of value and trust for your potential (and existing) customers.

In fact, three of the biggest mistakes made by small businesses are:

1. Not taking the time to figure out the fluffy, but important stuff.

Their beliefs, values, mission, purpose for existing, the emotional responses they want to create, and their long term impact.

2. Not being consistent.

Changing their branding often because 'they can.' Not having an intentional brand, thus leading to inconsistency across channels. Not being specific enough and trying to be too many things to too many people with the limited resources they do have.

3. Not valuing design and aesthetics.

Steve Jobs said, "Design is not just what it looks like and feels like. Design is how it works." In the case of your branding, it's the emotions and psychological cues that your brand evokes.

There are three main parameters you should keep in mind when deciding if a design is good or not:

1. It evokes emotion.

What are the emotions that the design brings up when you and your potential customers look at it? Are these emotions relevant to what you're trying to achieve?

2. It's functional.

Can it be used with a variety of different materials? Or is it too complex to print?

3. It's a status symbol.

It needs to represent the value you're offering to your customers, the thing that helps them improve their lives. This is usually developed over time as your brand establishes itself, but it is also something you can influence from the design aspect. A status symbol doesn't always mean luxury. Harley-Davidson, for example, has such a powerful brand that people will tattoo the logo on their bodies and proudly display it, saying to everyone, "I'm a Harley guy/gal." That's powerful.

Developing Your Brand Book

One of the best ways to ensure your brand is being accurately represented is to develop a brand book or a manual of how to use the elements of your brand. It's a simple document that provides the necessary explanations and instructions on how to handle each element—the logo, colors, images and message. This is something that can be prepared very early on. In fact, the sooner, the better. This doesn't mean you can't change it, or that the visual elements of your company will stay as they are specified in the book forever; it just means that whoever needs to coordinate or execute any creative work, be it with colors, design, or words, can use the brand book as a guide to know what is allowed and what isn't, then build from there.

But, preparing any kind of document, and especially a specific one such as a brand book can be quite overwhelming. So, what should it include? Let's expand on some of the visual elements.

Your Brand's Design Elements

The thing that first pops into one's head when talking about visual elements is design. These elements can be combined in an infinite number of ways, giving you an opportunity to come up with a design that is unique to your company, your message, and that resonates with your Perfect Client.

1. Logo + Icons

We attach meaning to symbols such as logos, but they in and of themselves don't mean much. Since the early days of civilization, humans have used symbols to represent things ranging from social status to their belief systems. Your icons can be as simple as your packaging: the awesome feeling when you get an Amazon box at your doorstep or pull out a new Apple product from its packaging. Or they can be as complex as personas you create: like Geico's Gecko, Flo from Progressive, Ronald McDonald, Tony The Tiger from Frosted Flakes, or Nike's athletes that represent the greatness of the human body. These are all iconic things unique to each brand.

The simplest form of an icon is your logo. A logo is the graphic representation of the brand, it's the first thing the audience—existing and potential customers—might notice. And once the brand is well known, it can exist on its own, without having to complete it with the name. Just think of Nike—you don't need to see the name of the brand to relate the tick to the company and its products, along with the emotions associated to it.

Just an interesting side note: these are three of the most expensive rebrands and logo design projects:

1. **BP**: $211,000,000 in 2008

2. **Pepsi**: $1,000,000 in 2008

3. **BBC**: $1,800,000 in 1997

And here are three of the cheapest logos:

1. **Google: $0**. The original logo was designed by Sergey Brin, Google co-founder in 1998.

2. **Coca Cola: $0**. John Pemberton's bookkeeper, Frank Mason Robinson, came up with the name and created the logo in 1885. John Pemberton was an American pharmacist and the founder of Coca Cola.

3. **Nike: $35**. Phil Knight paid graphic design student Carolyn Davidson in 1975 to design the logo.

So don't go spending millions on a logo, but if you do, call us and we'll do it for $500k. Jokes aside, a logo is crucial in creating brand consistency but I wouldn't spend too much time agonizing on making it perfect. Your logo can evolve as your business evolves and you can create a beautiful logo quickly, or hire someone to do it for you. If you're still choosing a logo or going through a rebrand, there are three ways to approach the design of it:

Iconic / Symbolic

The icon/symbol represents the brand. The most common examples that come to mind are those of Apple, Nike, or, for example, the Olympic Games circles. They have so much history and smart marketing behind them that they are practically living on their own and are, in fact, legendary. Again, these symbols rarely have meaning early on, it's the rest of the brand elements working together along with the value you create that gives these symbols meaning.

Logotype / Wordmark

Think of Amazon or Google, where the font and the color of the name make the logo. When these appear as logos, there's only one way they can be used. But, what's more, the fonts used have become so well known that most people recognize them in a heartbeat even if they're used to write something completely different. Just think of the Coca Cola font: even if you use it to write your address, you'll still be reminded of one of the most (if not the most) famous soft drinks of all times.

Combination Logo

Combining the icon/symbol with the specific design of the name. This is usually my favorite because in most cases it makes it clear to people what you do. Two very good examples of this type of logo are Starbucks or Under Armour, they both have unique typography and a unique symbol. These two main elements, the design of the brand name and the icon/symbol, complement each other. Each element can stand alone or be used together.

Whatever type your logo is, what's most important is that it is always applied in the same way in terms of proportions (if you're combining different elements), using the same font, colors, design, icon/symbol, and background combination. All of this information needs to be included in the brand book in as many ways as possible, with actual examples of correct and incorrect usage.

Whenever your business is represented, the logo should be present and visible, so it slowly generates recognition among your potential and existing customers, and gradually comes to occupy that very desirable bit of space in their memory for your brand to live in. In the end, without the clear message, values, and identity to accompany the logo, it is just an icon or a beautifully designed word/name.

2. Colors

Your logo and brand name need to live in an environment of colors that are consistent with the logo, with the product or service you offer, as well as the context of your campaigns.

The colors you choose to represent your brand, along with the logo and the brand name, will be used in all of the online marketing materials, from the website, banners, profile materials you use on different social networks, etc, and it all needs to work together, function as a whole, and represent your business appropriately.

Each color has a different impact and what works for some businesses might not work for yours. For example, just because a party venue makes excellent use of combining purple and black, and has great success, it doesn't mean that these colors will work for an attorney. The context of each industry is very different, and the colors should represent them accordingly.

Studies have shown that blues give a calming and trusting feeling, while reds raise the adrenaline levels and heart rate. It's part of the reason why in healthcare you see a lot of neutral and blue hues.

When we're selecting colors and creating a brand color palette, we **try to stick to 2-3 colors max**. This allows us to be flexible when we start introducing full color photography and other media that enriches the brand.

Base Color
This is the dominant color and we usually go with a more neutral color. Shades of white, gray, black, beiges or browns, otherwise bright, dark or neutral colors.

Accent Color
This is the pop of color that makes your brand stand out.

A Third Color
If we want a third color, we'll either find colors similar to our accent color, just varied in hue, saturation or brightness. Complimentary colors work well to give you that added pop. This is especially important when creating buttons on web pages or calls to actions on marketing materials.

Once you have your colors selected, make sure you write down the exact color codes you're using. You'll need to know the color values such as CMYK (for anything printed) and RGB (for anything on a screen or web). Any good graphic designer should be able to provide you with this information, but should you have any doubts, there are websites that can convert the colors from one color "language" to another.

3. Fonts

Once you have your logo and colors, another important aspect that you should consider and that brings everything together is consistency in font choice.

▷ A **serif** font, like the Rolex logotype or fashion brands, can represent luxury, timelessness, and prestige.

▷ A **sans-serif** font, like the Google logotype and other technology companies, can symbolize modern, progressive qualities.

SANS / SERIF

Sans ("to be without") Serif fonts do NOT have any flourishes at the end of the strokes.

A **serif** is a small *decorative flourish* on the end of the end of the strokes that make up letters and symbols.

These don't need to be particularly innovative, but they do need to match your overall identity (no Comic Sans for an attorney's office), they need to be consistent internally (memos, internal documents, and presentations), and externally (emails, the font on the website, the font used on the images you post on your social media).

The brand book should specify exactly what these situations are and how each font should be used (size, color, position in relation to other elements, etc).

By having these three—logo, colors and fonts—defined, you and your team will have fewer difficulties being consistent when it comes to representing your brand in a visual manner.

4. Photography, Video And Image Style

With the design defined and explained in the brand book, the next thing to think about is media. Proper use of media makes your brand tangible and starts to create that emotional connection we're looking for. Nothing conveys the excellent service of a dentist better than the beautiful, happy and authentic smile of a girl on a Facebook post or magazine ad.

Hiring a professional photographer.

I recommend small businesses get at least one professional photography session done per year. There's nothing better than original photography to use across all your marketing. A great photographer will be able to help you tell your business story and will pay for themselves over the course of a year. Just call a local photographer and ask how much their day rates are, and that you're a small business looking for help. More often than not, they're super happy to help and will shoot during the week.

Using stock photos.

However, for some projects, you don't need a photo session every time you need images to use with your brand on social media or in brochures/flyers. There are image banks that can be purchased and some places are even free.

Our favorite places for paid stock photos are:

1. Shutterstock. https://www.shutterstock.com/
2. Graphic Stock. https://www.graphicstock.com
3. iStockPhoto. http://www.istockphoto.com/

You can also check out these places for free stock photos:

1. Unsplash. https://unsplash.com/
2. Stock Snap. https://stocksnap.io/
3. Pexels. https://www.pexels.com/

Use Your Smartphone.
With a bit of general understanding of composition, distribution of elements, lighting and colors, anyone in possession of a smartphone with a decent camera can take pictures to be used for online media. The iPhone 7 has a phenomenal portrait mode camera to take awesome photos of people and close ups of objects. Using your smartphone to take original images for social media on a consistent basis helps build your brand tremendously.

And these can truly make a difference. Just think of all the pictures plastic surgeons, dentists, attorneys-at-law, or real estate agents use to communicate with potential customers. Is there better proof of the quality of their services than photos of the finished products and other happy customers?

When not to go cheap on your media.
However, there are some images and video where quality is non-negotiable. These are the ones that have a longer 'shelf life' and that will be used over and over again. We're referring to things like your team's headshots, shots of your facilities, your product photography and things that you'll otherwise use across multiple channels. For these we definitely recommend you hire a professional to deliver high-quality pictures or videos.

Why? Because people will inevitably judge you by how you and your company look. And having poorly lit photos, shaky videos and awkward angles can damage the overall image of your company. If you do yearly photoshoots, it shows your customers that you're active, that you care about your company's image and the quality you produce. The way you treat yourself will be a great indicator of trust to your customers, as they will be certain they can expect the same quality of service before they even step into your business.

Starbucks does a fantastic job of this in their stores. Their photography speaks volumes about their product. From shots of their coffee, their farmers, and the different cities around the world, they all contribute to the overall experience of your cup of coffee.

5. The Experience Your Customers Have With Your Business.

Starbucks wants their coffee shops to smell like coffee. They have outlets and wifi for you to bring your laptop to work, meet with people and create.

Compare that to the Nespresso brand of coffee, Nestle's high end coffee brand. You can find boutique kiosks in luxury department stores like Bloomingdales where they'll make you a free gourmet cup of coffee while they showcase their individual 'pods' and espresso machines. Nestle also makes instant coffee, which people pay a few cents for per cup, but Nespresso is far from that, and their customers are far from the instant-coffee type.

The Nespresso Beverly Hills Boutique & Cafe on Beverly Drive often has exotic cars parked out front, and when you arrive, a hostess greets you and will take you to your seat, much like a formal restaurant would, and that's if there isn't a wait. Regardless of whether you transact online or offline, your customers' experience has a profound effect on how they view your brand. Sometimes this experience often has very little to do with your actual product or service. This experience is what must be intentionally designed by you.

6. Your Message

We typically start here when we're developing a brand. Your message is something that needs to be intentionally designed and consistently communicated verbally and in written form. Without a clear message, the other elements are random and have little lasting effect on your audience. Each brand has a message to communicate, one that identifies it and separates it from its competitors. It should be clear and easy to remember to make it as memorable as possible.

Confused people don't buy.

If you can't articulate your value proposition in a tweet, it's most likely too complicated. When things are complicated, confusing or esoteric, it won't break through the noise of the marketplace, and even if it does, it won't be remembered by your audience.

Your brand's message complements the other elements and should be used consistently in all your communications, from your website to your social media profiles. It will, if communicated correctly and coherently, convince them to give you and your business a chance. The visual elements might grab your prospects' attention, but your message will persuade them to start the journey across The Bridge.

Start with why.

My favorite approach to crafting a compelling message comes from Simon Sinek's TED Talk: "How great leaders inspire action." Most of us have answers to the questions of what we do and how we do things, but it's a lot harder to answer why we do things. Simon looked at the greatest companies and leaders, then analyzed how they communicated.

He noticed that they communicated radically different (from the inside out as he calls it in his Golden Circle concept). Apple started with phrases like, "We believe..." and highlighted their arduous process for achieving beautiful and functioning products. Compare that to their competitors, who talked about gigabytes of ram and processing speeds. Apple's approach has proved to inspire and attract people who believe what they believed.

The easiest way to go about it is to simply ask yourself why you do what you do. Then ask it again. Then ask it again. And again, until you reach the fundamental truth of why you do the things you do. Why you started your business, why you work day in and day out to perfect your craft.

I believe entrepreneurs are wired to solve problems. If I can help more entrepreneurs succeed, we can solve a lot more of the problems in the world. This book is a part of that. When I dig even deeper, my why is that entrepreneurship allowed me to become more than what society thought I could do, because of where I came from and my situation growing up.

I believe business forces you to go beyond yourself, your self interests and needs, in order to serve others and create value. That's something that's very hard to learn anywhere else.

I believe entrepreneurship to be a journey of personal discovery and development. In order to better serve others you must first become more than you currently are.

Communicating this way has helped me create a personal brand, a movement, and a company that people want to work with. From our team to our clients, we all believe parts of this philosophy. This why is real, authentic, and true to who I am. It's not fabricated for the purposes of a marketing campaign.

All the relevant messages will be built on this foundation. Your website text, your core values, your mission, your value proposition, everything in your marketing and everything that is used at your company on a daily basis. Once you write it down, it will become a reality to adhere to, and not just some concept floating around the office.

The brand goes beyond just your customers. Your team needs to identify with it as well, they need to have a shared sets of beliefs, the same goals and missions. Maybe not 100%, since in the end we are all different, but when it comes to representing your company, you need to be on the same page.

The only way to do that is to be very clear about what your brand stands for, how it should be represented visually, and what the main messages to convey are. By being clear and passionate about these, people will work harder than anybody towards your company's success, and you'll start to attract your Perfect Client Profile.

Get A *FREE* Video Deep-Dive Training here:
clientacquisitionblueprint.com/freegift
($297 Value, Yours *FREE*)

Building Your Website

CHAPTER 3

How to build an asset online that serves as the foundation for your online marketing.

If your business is not on the internet, it's almost as if it doesn't exist. Having an online presence is essential, and it starts with the website: the virtual home of your brand and the foundation of your business.

When it comes to websites, one of the biggest mistakes people make is simply in the way they choose to approach it. A business website is much more than a flyer on the web. Just a beautiful website to look at won't get you any customers—it should have a clearly communicated purpose and drive people to take action.

Your website is also not just a place for customers to find information about your products and services or read your fluffed-up bio.

Your website should be your biggest business asset online. An asset that's growing, that's getting quality visitors (traffic) daily, and that's turning those visitors into qualified prospects. As such, it should be worked on, developed, invested in, and checked on constantly so it can evolve and grow with your business and the market. You must also have a system to follow up with those prospects and educate them towards a decision of doing business with you. On a foundational level, your website serves three primary functions.

1. **Establish trust and credibility** in the mind of potential customers.

2. **Turn traffic into leads for your business**—we'll discuss this in more detail in the Conversion and Automation chapters.

3. **Make you money**—yes, make money directly on your website, even if you don't run an ecommerce brand or your business provides services and requires formal contracts or letters of engagement. A well thought out, designed and implemented website with a clear purpose and message can, in fact, make you money on its own.

Let's start with the basics first. Here are three elements your website must have to achieve its primary functions.

3 MUST-HAVE ELEMENTS FOR YOUR WEBSITE

1. Persuasive and Compelling Copy
2. Clean, Modern, Mobile Design
3. Simple Search Engine Optimization (SEO)*

Compelling Copy: Text That Embodies Who You Are and Attracts Your Perfect Client Profile

We've been doing some of this work since the first two chapters, but here's where you start to actually write your message. Website

---

* So your website and business can be found online.

text is usually referred to as copy. Copy refers to the output of copywriters, or writers whose focus is to write material which encourages people to buy your products, goods or services.

The website is the perfect place to present your business and the value you offer to your audience. It's one of the few online channels where the communication is unidirectional and completely decided by you.

Therefore, it's essential to take advantage of this opportunity and work on copy that clearly transmits the essence of your business to your customers. It is where your unique selling proposition should be clearly stated for the world to see.

This copy should communicate in a way that your website's visitors can relate to. When working on the text, imagine you're talking directly to your perfect customer. What words would you use to convince them? What tone? Would the text be long or shorter? In the Conversion Pages chapter (Chapter 7) we'll cover some simple copywriting formulas that increase your conversions and maximize your results.

But by answering these questions, you can work on text that will give you the results you're looking for in the long run. And if the copy you worked so hard on doesn't seem to work, don't worry—you can always change it! This is one of those things that you test, test, and test. Even if it's working, you can always improve.

Clean, Modern, Mobile Design

When it comes to the design of the website, it should be attractive but clean so it doesn't distract visitors from the content and your message. The latest trend is a clean, minimalistic design, but when choosing the best option for your business, don't forget about the brand, the logo, the colors you've chosen, and any other graphic elements that complete it.

Your website should be perfectly displayed on all types of devices—desktops, laptops, tablets, and smartphones. Having a responsive design is a must, especially taking into consideration that tablets and smartphones are, more often than not, the devices of choice when it comes to searching for information online. The information should be easily accessible and readable from all devices and at all times.

If you're not really tech-savvy or if this is all brand new to you, where do you begin? You have the brand thought out, the message defined, you know how you want it done, but how do you get it from your head to the browsers of potential customers?

What To Build Your Website With

The first question to address should be: where? On what platform should you build your website? Here are three basic choices to choose from:

1. Custom built website

This is basically a website that's built from scratch for the purposes of your business. This is usually the approach big companies with big budgets take, as it takes a team of developers and designers working together. It is especially used if you'd also like to incorporate ecommerce or any other "beyond-just-information" elements. And while it's amazing to have a unique website exactly as you want it, the investment it requires can quickly reach sky-high limits, not to mention it's much more expensive to maintain once it's launched. From what I've seen, a fully custom website will cost you at least $25,000 for something basic, but I've seen clients come to us after spending $100k+. For 95% of businesses, this is simply not necessary.

2. WordPress

This is the option most small businesses (and even big businesses) are choosing, and for several very clear reasons: WordPress is simple enough to understand, change, and modify.

While it used to have its limitations in terms of design possibilities, there are now thousands of different customizable templates on sites like Themeforest and Elegant Themes, with even more plugins to complement them and increase their functionality. It's becoming easier and easier to get the website exactly as desired in a shorter period of time. If you can't build it yourself, hiring a web designer, developer or agency won't cost you tens of thousands of dollars for the website alone. It's also the most popular platform at the moment, meaning it's the most supported, so whatever the issue, it's now really easy to fix.

3. DIY Website Builders

These options, such as Squarespace, are similar to WordPress and can be customized to your liking, but they're just not as flexible. Unlike Wordpress, where you can have a developer install it on your own hosting and actually access the coded files, a lot of builders limit your access to their development tools. This option is great if you want a simple website to just showcase your work, products or services. Companies like Shopify allow you to build your own ecommerce sites and have fantastic support.

Other options include Drupal, Joomla or Wix are platforms that had their "15 minutes of fame" but dropped off the radar since and have not been innovating as much recently. New things show up on the market all the time, so it's best to find a platform that is stable, has been around for a few years, and has a large user base. That way you don't risk having your website become obsolete.

Who Should You Trust With
Your Business Asset?

The first question goes hand in hand with the second one—who? Who should you entrust with your website? One of the only shortcuts I've taken in business is this: find people to help, not only do stuff for me, but teach me about the process.

Whether it's an attorney, accountant or my business coach, I've surrounded myself with people with exceptional expertise and the willingness to teach. I'd encourage you to do the same with your marketing. Find someone to take the journey with you, help you do stuff, and teach you what they know. It doesn't mean they're teaching you so you can do it yourself, it simply allows you to grow and improve as a business owner. It allows you to avoid mistakes and maximize your efforts. At the very least, it allows you to have intelligent conversations with people and manage projects better.

While you can definitely choose the best option for building your site, you can also use the expertise of the people that will be working on your website to give you their recommendation based on your specific needs, requirements and expectations.

So, when it comes to who can build your website, the options are quite clear.

Freelancers

There are great online platforms, such as Upwork.com or Freelancer.com, where you can search for freelance help. You could also reach out to any fellow small business owners and ask them for the contact info of the person who worked on their website.

This is usually the most affordable option, making it the most attractive for most small business owners, but it's also a risky one. Yes, there are some extremely professional freelancers out there who will work on your project with the same passion you do, but there are also some that might disappear, overestimate their capacities, have limited access to resources (such as graphic designers, writers, etc), and can sometimes leave the website only half-finished. It's a common complaint I hear about web designers. They go MIA when they're stretched too thin or take on more projects than they can deliver on.

If this is the way you decide to go, make sure you search for as many references as you can on the freelancer to get a very good notion of what to expect and be aware that there is a chance it might not work out perfectly the first time around. But if you find the hidden gem and build a relationship with them, they can provide you with outstanding results and grow as your business grows.

Agencies

These are your marketing agencies, web design agencies, or design studios. Try to find one that is focused mainly on small businesses rather than using small businesses as a stepping stone to get bigger clients.

An agency will usually have either full time team members to work on your project, or access to vetted freelancers for more advanced stuff. If there are any special aspects to your website, they can take the load off you in finding the best way to solve it. There are also many that specialize in a certain type of business, meaning they know the market and what works best, based on their own experience and what their other clients have shared with them.

And while a freelancer is someone that needs to be managed, with a good agency you can hand over the work and do regular check-ins to see the progress. A good agency will provide you with guidance and strategy. They are usually more expensive than an average freelancer, but not nearly as much as some of the biggest marketing agencies.

As with hiring any vendor, make sure to check out their past work, reviews, and ask for references if you feel you need to. Start with a small project if you can to make sure you're able to work well together. That way when the big projects come along, you'll have some common ground and your brands assets ready to go.

Industry Specific Agencies

Aside from the smaller agencies (usually a group of marketing and creative individuals), you'll often see larger marketing agencies or companies that only serve your industry. This is common in dentistry, real estate, accounting and pretty much every industry.

Though it may be a great choice to go with them in the beginning, oftentimes you need a slightly more custom solution. It doesn't make sense for your website to have the exact same template and copy as 7,000 other dentists. Even if they say they have multiple designs and can develop custom things for you, chances are you'll still end up looking like your competition. I recommend finding someone you like working with and can build your relationship with for years to come.

These industry-specific agencies also often have closed systems and they actually own your website. When you decide to cancel with them, they don't hand over your website. Even if they gave you access to a dashboard to change a few things on your site, you don't own or really control your website. Thus, you're never building a real asset.

Big Agencies

These often boast client lists of Fortune 500 companies they've worked with. But the way you market a multinational corporation is different than marketing a bootstrapped business. They usually want to be shooting Super Bowl commercials and winning awards rather than getting results and helping a business make money.

However, regardless of who you choose to build your website, make sure they have the knowledge and understanding of:

1. Marketing, business, and growth strategies that work.

2. Great design and branding principles.

3. Creating a great user experience.

4. The technical aspects of your website—programming, databases, security, hosting, etc.

As a small business owner, there are other things for you to focus on that don't include trying to figure out WordPress and how to master it on your own. Find someone you like working with and that can deliver results for your business. Have him/her guide you through the process so that by having this basic understanding, you'll be able to provide valuable suggestions and not start from the very beginning if you ever need to change the agency or freelancer.

For more detailed and up-to-date info on
building a website, visit:
clientacquisitionblueprint.com/freegift

Simple And Well-Thought SEO
So People Can Find You In Searches

The majority of your website's visitors will come through the biggest search engines—Google, Yahoo! and Bing—and it's obviously crucial that your website appear among the relevant results on all of these search engines.

Simply having your website built and live doesn't mean people will automatically find it. It's important to consider SEO when starting your web development project and urge whoever is building it to follow basic SEO practices so you don't have to go back and start from scratch.

You can have good search ranking (this practice is known as Search Engine Optimization, or SEO) with a few simple steps. The first one is definitely to think about the words and expressions your potential customers would use to search for a product or service like yours, and then make sure you use them across the copy/text on your site. These words, known as keywords, should be at the beginning of the website and used throughout. This is where the engines begin the reading. The closer to the beginning, the better. Don't assume Google or your visitors will know what your website is about.

Use text to describe the visual elements of the website, such as images and videos. Search engines cannot know the content of a video, but they can read the short and to-the-point description you use. This is often referred to as meta-data.

Determining your keyword and ranking strategy is a fundamental step to being found in searches. Potential customers will typically search something in one of these three keyword strategies:

1. **Brand keywords**: These are keywords that relate to your brand, such as your company name, your founder's name and key people.

2. **Industry keywords**: These are the keywords related to your product, service or industry.

3. **Local search**: What cities do you want to target? With more searches coming from local and mobile search when people are using their phones, it's important to target the specific cities and locations where your customers live and shop.

The structure of your website and its pages is also a very important aspect of SEO. Your website needs to have a logical structure and all of the content on it should be easily accessible (how many clicks does it take to get to the most "hidden" piece of content on your website?).

Finally, there are the *meta tags*, such as *meta robots* and *meta descriptions*—the descriptions behind the visible content (what the search engines read)—which can mark the difference when talking about good SEO. These are a bit more technical, but if your website is built on WordPress, you can search for SEO plugins. Most of them already include spaces for them to make it as easy as possible to add. Your agency or freelancer should also be able to help you with basic SEO. The goal of this section is simply to remind you and give you a framework for thinking about SEO.

CASE STUDY

How a florist went from making bouquets in his basement to opening a waterfront location in Seattle, increasing his fees 5x, and winning awards as the #1 florist in his market.

The Problem

Let's close this chapter with a case study of a client of ours, a florist in Seattle, Washington. He did some high-profile weddings in Los Angeles, but after moving to Seattle, he was forced to start all over again, literally making his floral arrangements in his basement. His dream was to continue working high-end weddings, but it was clear as day that he had to be strategic with his marketing since people couldn't visit his shop in the basement.

The Solution

A simple strategy and message, a great brand, a professional-looking website where clients could see his work, and beautiful pictures from different weddings he worked. Because of his website, he was admitted into a prestigious wedding show and began building his business. He now has a waterfront location in Seattle because he was able to present himself differently online, and people judged him based on his online presence and not his actual place of work.

Getting Your Business on the Global Map

CHAPTER 4

The online accounts and profiles that give your business maximum exposure.

Having a website is not the only thing you need to do to establish a solid online presence. If you want to reach the next level, the next step forward is to have online accounts or profiles that literally put your business on the map. Here's a great example to emphasize the importance of having online accounts or profiles, but first...

A Quick Warning

Small business owners usually start feeling overwhelmed or bored at this point. After all, this isn't why you got into business. You got into business to do something you love and make great money doing it. But in order to do that, you need customers that allow you to do your best work, as was the case with Bob, an auto mechanic I worked with.

Bob had to relocate his auto repair shop after 30 years due to a huge spike in his rent. He was a great guy, did great work, and his clients loved him. But needless to say, the change cost him the vast majority of his clientele—they simply weren't willing to make the drive in LA traffic to see him.

The once thriving, steady business was now a distant memory. His old clients looked for options closer to their homes or work, and with other established and well-known auto repair shops around, he barely made ends meet month after month.

What makes Bob interesting is that, unlike many of his competitors, he sets fair prices, treats people well, is very good at what he does and he just loves doing it. Cars are his life, and he'll take care of each vehicle that arrives at his shop as if it were his own. The quality of his work in undeniable and the few customers he does have are extremely satisfied with his service.

For 30 years, Bob never really had to market his business. He had followed the blueprint of "build it and they will come." It worked then, it didn't work now.

In today's world of unlimited options, where finding any kind of business on the internet is just one or two clicks away, auto repair shops included, Bob was missed in the crowd more often than not.

Just a Google search was enough to see that his repair shop was not easy to find. The profiles of his business were not consistent, the information was different and mainly incomplete from one to another, making his shop appear less appealing and trustworthy than other repair shops nearby. That is, if his shop showed up at all – to find him online, a specific "Bob's Auto Repair Shop" search was necessary, and even then, listings he had created with "Bob's Mechanic Shop" and "B&B Mechanics" all added to the confusion.

I sat there walking him through how to log in to his accounts, resetting his passwords, and explaining different dashboards and platforms to him. As we were doing this, he became increasingly frustrated with the technology and complained, "I don't want to do this. I just want to work on cars."

So, why should Bob, a man in his late 50s who just wants to fix cars and earn an honest living, invest time and energy trying to fix his local listings? Because it's not about his local listings. It's about his disposition and willingness to do whatever it takes to succeed and save his failing business.

He wasn't just complaining about his passwords, he was shooting every marketing idea down because he'd simply never had to learn it or do any marketing at all. It's no easy task to learn the basics of a brand new craft, even more so if this craft is not appealing for the person. Regardless, digital marketing is a practice that can be learned, and the benefits of implementing some very basic techniques and tools will be well worth his time.

How My Dad's Paint Poisoning Forced Him To Learn New Skills And Start A Business

Bob is an immigrant from Eastern Europe, and working with him reminded me of my dad. My dad was a painter, painting buildings and homes for the majority of his life. His education ended in the 3rd grade of elementary school, after which he entered the workforce in Mexico in search of a better life. When he migrated to the US, his jobs were always manual labor. His latest career had him working with oil based paints and very little protection.

One day, after years of being exposed to toxic chemicals, he got paint poisoning. This had lasting damaging effects on his health. He was unable to tolerate strong odors, he lost his strength, lost weight, had respiratory and neurological damage, and just getting through the day proved to be incredibly challenging.

With my dad unable to work and provide for our family, I had to become head of household at 18. For the next 2½ years, I worked a sales job, went to community college, and learned media and design by watching Youtube videos. I could see my dad begin feeling like he was losing his identity and worrying about what he was going to do. His whole life was wrapped up in providing for his family through manual labor, and now he was unable to even tolerate the scent of someone cooking.

As I watched Youtube videos on how to design in Photoshop, shoot photography, and edit videos, I taught my dad what I was learning. He had never used a computer before and he barely knew how to read and write English. Everything in the software we were using was in English and all the tutorials online were also in English.

He resisted at first, but he knew that this could be valuable to him and he had to figure out a new way to provide for his family. Manual labor and his previous career were no longer an option.

Within 12 months of us working together, he learned photography, video, and even got his first few paying clients shooting Quinceañeras and weddings. He learned how to edit photos in Adobe Lightroom, do graphic design in Photoshop, and use Final Cut Pro to edit videos.

My dad now has a thriving business in the Seattle area, earning him more than he ever earned before. He felt a duty and responsibility to figure it out, for our family and for his dignity and sense of self worth.

The same thing applies to marketing. If it's a bit uncomfortable or you find it boring, hang in there. Find someone to guide you. Ask other business owners. Start with one piece of The Client Acquisition Blueprint and build from there.

We took a break from Bob's account setup and I told him my dad's story. It inspired him to keep working on his marketing and moving forward. If my dad, with a 3rd grade education and very little English, could start a thriving business, you can figure out this marketing stuff.

If Bob dedicates an hour per week to focus on the marketing of his business, unifies his online profiles, asks for referrals, and makes sure the necessary information is online and easy to find, his auto repair shop will have a much better chance of survival. More people will find him, meaning there will be a greater chance of attracting a bigger number of customers to visit his repair shop and entrust him with their cars. However, without the online profiles, without the online presence, the chances of improvement are next to none.

Local Listing Sites

Long gone are the days of the yellow pages being delivered to your front step, but the concept behind them is still in use today. The local listing sites index small businesses, mainly according to geography and category, so when your potential customers use these websites or apps to search for your services, your business will be displayed as the best nearby option for them.

Having your business on the local listing sites, such as Yelp, Google My Business, Bing, Yahoo!, Foursquare, etc can bring additional exposure and increased traffic to your website. It will help your business appear even more professional and help you get better SEO, all of which are important elements that work together towards increasing your business visibility and allow you to reach your goals.

You might think of sites like Yelp as review sites only, or sites that are only used for restaurants, but they are far more powerful than that. Yelp actually feeds their business data to Apple Maps and other sites. They also work for consulting businesses, attorneys, doctors and pretty much any business that wants more customers. We've personally gotten clients worth $15,000+ from Yelp inquiries.

Industry Directories and Authority Sites

Just like the real estate industry has Zillow and Trulia, most industries have websites where customers look for goods and services. These are another type of listing sites, which are much more specialized. While the "local listing sites" work for every business, the Industry Directories and Authority sites are specific to an industry.

For example, a real estate agent should, without a doubt, be listed on Yelp and Google My Business, but it should also be listed on Zillow and Trulia. Every industry has either directory/listing websites or authority sites where people are searching for that specific service, product, or information.

Different Types of Listing Websites

There are different types of these websites, namely:

1. **Directories / Listings**. Think "online yellow pages."

2. **Professional Organizations**. Industry associations, networking groups, trade shows, BNI, etc.

3. **Authority Sites**. These are sites that produce and curate content. They post relevant industry content, videos, article, reviews, etc.

4. **Forums**. Websites like Quora.com and Reddit.com where people ask questions and anyone can answer. Sites like Quora usually have experts answering these questions with immense detail.

5. **Marketplaces**. Websites where people buy and sell services, like angieslist.com, thumbtack or even Zillow can be considered a marketplace.

6. **Social Media Sites**. We have a whole chapter on this in Chapter 5.

Here are some examples of these websites for specific industries. It's not an exhaustive list but it's a start:

1. **Healthcare**
   a. vitals.com
   b. healthgrades.com
2. **Plastic Surgeons**: realself.com

3. **Chiropractors**: spine-health.com

4. **Dentists**: ada.org

5. **Legal**
   a. avvo.com
   b. lawyers.com
   c. usattorneys.com
   d. findlaw.com

6. **Financial Advisors, Wealth Management**: plannersearch.org

7. **Accountants, Bookkeepers**
   a. Quickbooks Pro Advisors
   b. taxprofessionals.com

8. **Wedding Industry**
   a. weddingwire.com
   b. theknot.com
   c. weddings.com

9. **Expert Industry**—coaches, consultants, authors, speakers
   a. clarity.fm
   b. quora.com

10. **Publishing** on Amazon, iTunes, Barnes & Noble: goodreads.com

11. **Real Estate**:
    a. zillow.com
    b. trulia.com
    c. realtor.com

12. **Automotive**:
    a. cars.com
    b. autotrader.com
    c. dealerrater.com

Perhaps not all of these are relevant for your specific situation, but with a little Googling you should be able to make a list of sites where you could list your business or contribute with content.

Your main focus at this point should be to find a way to get your website and business listed. Even if you don't plan on doing a marketing campaign on the platforms, as long as you have your foot in the door, your business will start showing up and be easier to find.

The authority websites, especially, have already done a lot of the work for you. They've created relevant content for your perfect customer profile; they invest in marketing, SEO, and advertising to attract those potential customers; and they allow you to either:

1. **Get a free listing on their site**

2. **Contribute content**

3. **Advertise**: Most of these websites have advertising opportunities for businesses like yours.

In order to make the right decisions regarding where to appear and get the perfect combination of local listings and industry directories, you need to know how and where people interested in your services are searching. Consider reviewing where your direct and most successful competitors appear to get a few ideas and get started.

Just Being There Isn't Enough

Once you decide which websites, listings, and directories work best for your business, you need to make sure that the information you post is consistent across all of the chosen websites. The easiest thing to do is to follow this short checklist to make sure everything is in place:

1. Business Name
You might think it's a waste of space to mention this, but you would be surprised by how many companies are called one thing

on one website and something different on another (like Bob's Mechanic Shop and Bob Auto Mechanics). Make sure you always use the exact same business name, and if you decide to use the logo, it should always be the same one across all channels. *Remember— consistency is key!*

2. Website Link

Those who find your online profile need to know where they can get more information, so the link to your main website is a must! You might also make the link go to a custom conversion page you designed. More on conversion pages in Chapter 7.

3. The Services You Offer

Preferably in a neat list format, explicitly using the keywords you came up with when you were building your website.

4. Description

This is the perfect opportunity to present your Value Proposition. What is it that you do different (and better) and why should any potential customers choose you over your competition?

5. Contact Information And Hours

You'd think it's common sense, but many companies still don't list these very useful details on their online profiles. I see businesses with info@theirwebsite.com, yet that account is inactive or they forgot about it.

6. Call-to-Action

The goal is to get the visitor off the platform they're on and check you out, then convert into a lead. Many websites offer the possibility of incorporating a button (that can take the customer to your conversion site or website), but if that's not possible, a simple, short call to action with the link will do the magic as well.

Having your online listing profiles set up with enough information for your potential clients will further strengthen your website traffic, and in consequence, your opportunity to generate leads. You'll be able to get the message across to more people due to appearing more in organic searches (SEO), and the results, although slow at first, will eventually blow your mind. It's a little bit of effort that will help you go a very long way, build a sustainable business, and help you achieve your desired results.

This is just another piece of The Client Acquisition Blueprint, but all of these ten keys, when implemented and working together, will have a lasting effect on your business.

Once leads start coming in, you'll be able to predict your cash flow and revenue with much more accuracy. With less frustration and stress, you can focus more on what you love doing and provide even more value to your existing and future clients.

Your Social Media Execution Plan

CHAPTER 5

Knowing where to play, what accounts to have, and what your moves are on social media for long term success.

Social media has caused a seismic shift in marketing. Each platform can be an excellent bidirectional channel of communication, where companies of all sizes can broadcast their messages to a very wide audience, learn about their customers and interact with them. And, best of all—social media is much cheaper than traditional media, offering more opportunities to react to what the audience likes or dislikes. It also allows you to be proactive to respond to the needs of your customers.

Still, using social media efficiently is no easy task and it can feel like you're building your brand on shifting sand. For starters, there is a great number of social media channels to choose from and to use them all at a high level requires an incredible amount of time and effort. Why? Because you're communicating with humans and people can smell a selfish salesperson from a thousand miles away. That's what most people try to do on social. They try to just push and promote their stuff versus trying to add real value to a specific audience.

2 Biggest Myths
About Social Media Marketing

1. "It's always changing."

The fact is, real marketing fundamentals haven't changed. You're dealing with human beings, psychology, and behavior that we've exhibited since the beginning of civilization.

Yes, the platforms may change, and what existed just a few months ago doesn't exist today, and what exists today might not exist in a few years, but that doesn't mean you shouldn't invest your time, energy, and resources in social media.

Social media is where your people are at, it's where your potential clients are already having the buying conversations. Your job is to build The Bridge so they can enter into your world and start the journey with you.

2. "I have to be on every platform and I have to post several times a day on every platform."

False. You don't need to focus on every platform and drive yourself nuts trying to make your posts go viral every day. You should definitely have an account on every platform (it's free) and make it consistent with your brand, but you shouldn't stretch yourself too thin.

You just need to focus on delivering real value AND making real connections with people. One great connection on social media can change your life and business. Don't get distracted by the platform.

How I Met My Wife With A Single Facebook Post (Even Though She Never Saw That Post)

When I was first getting started as an entrepreneur, I knew that my current social setting was not where my Perfect Client was nor where I would find the most opportunities. The places I hung out, the small town I was in, was not going to get me to where I wanted to go.

So I packed my stuff and moved to LA, an area with more than 10x the amount of people. I had no clients, no family, and no idea how I was going to make money in LA. My grand masterplan? Go hang out at a coffee shop in Beverly Hills everyday, work from my laptop and try to talk to people until I made one connection.

Fortunately, I didn't have to sit in a coffee shop and wait, but my plan still worked. I put myself in an environment where I perceived there was massive opportunity and focused on creating value for others. I knew I was in an area with 10 million people and in my mind, I saw this as 10 million opportunities to add value. Though I wasn't sure how, I knew that if I added value, something good would happen and I would be able to build my business.

In 2012 I posted a graphic on Facebook that caught the attention of a current client, Peter Voogd. At the time, he was just starting his movement to inspire millennials and he needed help with building his brand and social media influence. He messaged me on Facebook, we met up for coffee, and five years later, Peter inspires millions of millennials every single month to pursue their dreams and not settle for the status quo.

That one connection I made on Facebook was part of what allowed me to not have to sit in a coffee shop and hustle to make connections. My first week in LA, Peter introduced me to Kevin Ward at a conference. Kevin is a Real Estate Trainer, also reaching millions with his success trainings, and he became one of my first clients in LA. Kevin also gave me free tickets to a Brendon Burchard personal development conference in San Jose.

And that conference is where I met my wife.

Ok, maybe it's a stretch to say that I met my wife with a single Facebook post because there was a lot that happened in between, but the story is true. To me, this clearly illustrates the power of connecting with people, regardless of the medium. I connected with Peter on Facebook, I connected with Kevin at a conference, I met my wife at another conference, I asked her out to coffee, then lunch, then dinner, and eventually, I asked her to marry me. Funny part is, my wife actually lived in LA, one mile from Beverly Hills.

The point I'm making—and I can't stress it enough— is simply this: *social media is a way to connect with people*. You don't need millions of followers to make your social media powerful or worth your time, all you need is to genuinely connect with the right people.

What Platforms Work Best For Your Business?

Each network, or platform as I most commonly refer to them, provides different benefits and different ways of connecting with people, which makes the task a little more elaborate. So, how do you know which ones you should focus on?

First of all, it's important to know which social networks are out there, what their purpose is, and how users usually interact on the platform. Below you can find a list of the most popular and widely used social networks with some details that can help you tailor the communication to the chosen social media platform and the people that use it.

The way I think of social media is like going to any real-life social setting. After all, it's called social media. It's nothing more than people engaging in a virtual social setting, uploading pieces of their lives and thoughts, in an effort to engage with other people.

If you're going to a social gathering, the environment and the people matter. I'll refer to this as context. Each social setting can be different and unique in its own way, and that's why they attract different people to them. Going to a grungy bar downtown with your best friend to chat about work is different than going to a formal restaurant with your family, a business networking event, or a 5-star hotel bar. You'd dress different, act different, if you approached strangers you'd approach them differently, and your motives would be different based on the environment.

As you'll start to see, each platform has pre-established norms you have to learn first before engaging, and they have a predominant type of demographic there. Your job is to figure out if you can help the people there, if they match your Perfect Client Profile, and if you're going to commit to adding value and making connections. Sometimes, you'll have to dig deeper and spend more time figuring things out, other times it may be pretty simple for you. Find the platform that makes you the most comfortable and the one your Perfect Client uses, master that platform first, then repeat.

The list below is here to help you get started or find one that you might not be using fully. In upcoming chapters, I'll share with you my framework for engaging, building authority, collecting leads and ultimately making money from the top platforms, including the fastest way to get results from social media.

Of course, as I mentioned earlier, please be aware of their ever-changing nature—these are the social media platforms that are most popular today. Tomorrow, in a week, a month, or a year, the situation might be completely different.

1. Facebook

The largest database of humans in history.

▷ Publicly traded company (NASDAQ)
▷ Users: 1.86 billion (4th quarter of 2016)
▷ 72% of all online US adults visit Facebook at least once a month
▷ There are 40 million active small business pages, 2 million of these pay for advertising on the Facebook Ads platform

Facebook is one of the most universal networks and it's hard to go wrong when deciding on the communication style. Speak in a language your customers can understand and as long as you are authentic, you'll make connections with people.

As such, it's suitable for most businesses out there—big or small, product or services oriented, virtual or with an office your clients can visit—regardless of the industry, you can find your space and your target audience on Facebook.

Facebook also boasts one of the most robust advertising platforms ever. Through its enormous database of people and its strategic partnerships with other data agencies, its ad platform allows you to target people based on countless factors such as recent behaviors, demographics (marital status, age, gender, location, income), and interests (brands they consume, topics they're interested in) to name a few categories. Since Facebook owns Instagram, it also allows you to run ads on Instagram right from the Facebook ads manager.

Facebook Live and Facebook videos have recently started to pick up and the trend of video content is predicted to continue.

Having a mix of organic content and paid advertising is essential for success on Facebook.

2. Instagram

  ▷ Acquired by Facebook in 2012 for $1 billion USD
  ▷ Users: 600 million (12/2016)
  ▷ Over 80 million photos are uploaded per day
  ▷ 90% of Instagram users are younger than 35
  ▷ The most popular social network for 32% of US teens

Instagram is a platform we've seen great success in industries like plastic surgery, design, speakers, and aesthetic-driven industries. Keep in mind that the images you post need to resonate with your audience, they need to be of good quality and transmit a simple message.

Since Instagram is very popular with the younger demographic, this is an especially great option if your target audience is in the "Instagram age range." Wedding planners, florists, fashion designers, health providers, etc. can see an almost immediate increase in their business after starting their Instagram efforts.

3. Twitter

▷ Users: 313 million active users, 1.3 billion accounts registered
▷ Instant microblogging, a.k.a. "tweeting" limited to 140 characters
▷ Average daily activity: 6,000 tweets/second
▷ Publicly traded company (NYSE)

The 140 character limit of a tweet means that your communication needs to be concise and to the point! And while these can be accompanied by images or videos, there's not enough space for any sort of rambling.

I personally like Twitter to help me curate content, tweet at people I want to connect with, and write short, witty phrases that I can later turn into Instagram quotes. Big companies have found that it's a great way to connect with their customers in real time. Twitter is a great place to stay up to date with current events and trending topics. It also happens to be Donald Trump's favorite social media platform.

Interesting side note: Jack Dorsey, founder and CEO of Twitter, is also founder and CEO of Square, the payment processing company offering a suite of online business services from payment processing (mobile and storefronts), payroll, appointment setting, invoices, and even lending. Square is also a publicly traded company on the NYSE.

4. LinkedIn

▷ Users: 450 million members, 100 million access the network on a monthly basis
▷ Over 1 million members published content on LinkedIn
▷ Only 17% of US small businesses use this network
▷ It's mostly used as a professional network
▷ Acquired by Microsoft for $26 billion in 2016. One year prior, in 2015, LinkedIn had acquired Lynda, an online learning service, for $1.5 billion.

5. LinkedIn Pulse

This allows you to write longer form articles/blogs right on their platform. You can also post status updates and share content much like you would on Facebook or even Twitter.

People usually check LinkedIn for professional networking, to search for professional advice, to look for their next dream job, or to find non-fluffed content. The content, while far from uptight, has a different tone on LinkedIn than on other social media. It's typically much more polished, grounded and serious.

Professionals such as real estate agents, lawyers, wealth managers, or anybody that needs to build a lot of credibility among their potential clients can reap great benefits from establishing a strong LinkedIn profile. If your business is primarily B2B—serving other businesses—it's also a great place to connect with people inside of larger organizations, such as middle managers or even C level executives.

6. Snapchat

▷　Users: 100 million
▷　The population using the app is usually younger than 35
▷　The "Millennial" network—7 out of 10 Snapchatters are Millennials

As one of the most recent and innovative networks, it has taken the younger population by storm. It is a network for fun and excitement, which allows for authentic and personalized communication while keeping it light with the many filters they offer.

The content people post here can be more raw, unedited, and in the moment, allowing your audience to get a behind-the-scenes look at your life or company. Compare this to the perfect, premeditated and well-posed images on Instagram that only show the highlights of your life.

Despite many migrating to Instagram after the launch of Instagram Stories, there are still many companies whose target audience is comprised mainly of young people, who are still very active on Snapchat.

6. Pinterest

▷ Users: 100 million active, 176 million registered accounts
▷ 42% of all online women use the platform
▷ 65% of pinned content comes from brand websites

Pinterest is all about inspiration. Imagine a world of visual boards that can be molded to the user's liking. This network is especially useful for any aesthetics-related business. Beauty salons, spas, florists, fashion, unique furniture, etc can let their work speak on its own, as well as get inspired for their future projects. It's also a great tool for curating content and creating mood boards. They also offer advertising on their platform.

7. YouTube

▷ Users: Over 1 billion
▷ Every minute, 300 hours worth of video content is uploaded
▷ Over 50% of visitors come from mobile devices
▷ 9% of US small businesses use YouTube
▷ YouTube overall, and even YouTube on mobile alone, reaches more 18-34 and 18-49 year-olds than any cable network in the U.S.

Online videos are more and more becoming the preferred method of consumption. Every day people watch hundreds of millions of hours on YouTube and generate billions of views. Why read a blog post if you can watch a video on the same subject? Being able to share advice, experiences, success stories, or simply a tour around the office will allow your company to connect with your audience in a way that not many other networks allow.

On YouTube, you can't really go wrong. Every company can find its place there, whether it's a serious attorney's office, a healthcare practitioner or a consultant. It's all about finding what you want to say and saying it in the most creative way to engage your viewers. With properly structured titles, descriptions, and keywords, YouTube videos tend to rank extremely well in searches.

8. Google+

- ▷ Users: around 300 million
- ▷ 13% of US small businesses use Google+
- ▷ Predominantly male network: 74% of Google+ users are men

Despite Google+ not being the most popular network, it is still very relevant due to its link to YouTube and, well, Google. Since Google switched to a single login for all their services like Gmail, Youtube, and Google Drive, your Google+ profile is linked to that same login.

The communication on Google+ doesn't need to be very specific in its style, much like Facebook and YouTube. I don't think anyone has really figured out how Google+ is supposed to work, not even Google. If anything, just making sure your profile is consistent and on brand is enough to start. For most businesses, this Google profile is your Google My Business and is essential to customers finding you online.

Where To Start

To make the best decision, you should know what the preferred social media channels of your Perfect Client are and which ones

Sources: investor.fb.com, about.twitter.com, youtube.com/yt/press/statistics.html
Brandwatch: 96 Amazing Social Media Statistics and Facts for 2016
Mediakix: Snapchat Statistics 2016 Marketers Need to Know
Expanded Ramblings: Google Plus Statistics
Statistic Brain: Google Plus Demographics Statistics

they use when searching for a service or a product. Do they ask friends on Facebook? Do they engage with brands on Instagram? Are they reading articles on LinkedIn Pulse or looking for mutual connections to do business with? All of them? By answering these questions, you'll be able to narrow down your selection and direct your efforts to where they can actually yield results.

Though earlier I said you don't have to post on every platform every day, don't make the mistake of focusing so much on just one channel that you ignore the others. Social media profiles don't require any payment to be created, and the more you're present over the internet, the better. Find a mix that works for you to connect with your target audience on as many levels as possible.

In fact, if it's a new business or brand, one of the first things that we do once our clients decide on their company's name is to secure the name across all social media, regardless of which ones they end up using. This way, if at some point you'd like to experiment with a network that you haven't considered before, you'll already have the profile named exactly as it should be, and consistent with the rest of your online and social profiles.

Remember: when it comes to your brand, consistency and authenticity are key—and this applies to social media as well. Your usernames and URLs should be the same across all social media, so spending some time researching what's available is beyond recommended. And once you have those set up, the cover art, profile images, and value proposition should be consistent across all of your profiles.

> **REMEMBER**
>
> When it comes to your brand, consistency and authenticity are key—and this applies to social media as well.

Though we briefly covered this earlier, and we'll cover it in the Getting Attention section of the book, another thing to keep in mind is that the content will change depending on the social media channel. For example, Instagram is only visual, with fun images and short videos that display the product or service you offer in a highly aesthetic way. These can also be more casual and even lifestyle shots (showcasing your personal lifestyle or company culture). LinkedIn is much more professional, where you can use more text and even write professional articles and showcase your expertise. On Facebook, a channel that's much more personal at times, you can share your own content or content created by others that relates to your business, like videos, images, GIFs, etc. If you enjoy producing fun videos, a YouTube channel might be the way to go, and so on.

If after you work with a few channels it turns out you didn't get it quite right the first time around, don't worry! You can simply try a different platform with little to no additional cost. In fact, even professional marketers and media giants sometimes struggle when trying to figure out the latest trends and understanding which direction the market is moving. So, while there might be quite a bit of trial and error, the rewards of a consistent image and fast interaction with your potential clients (even if it's just a small fraction of them) will be worth more than you could ever imagine or sometimes even measure.

Whatever your mix of social media, your brand identity and the industry you're in, what is extremely important is that you remain authentic. Your social media presence needs to be as transparent and true to what your business represents as possible. And while it's possible to create a polished image using professionally produced media, by using Facebook Live, Instagram Stories or Snapchat, you can showcase the raw and unfiltered side of you and your business. Your audience will very quickly get a good sense of how authentic you're being, and reward (or punish) you accordingly with their attention, likes, comments, and shares.

How Elon Musk Fixed A Customer Complaint On Twitter In Six Days

Tesla provides free charging to their customers at their Supercharging stations and it notifies them on their phones when their cars are fully charged.

A customer @mentioned Elon Musk in a tweet on December 10, 2016 regarding people leaving their Teslas in the Supercharger slots, even after they were fully charged as if it were a parking space:

This would be like arriving at a packed gas station only to see people using the gas pumps as parking spots while they grabbed lunch or got work done at Starbucks.

6 days later—yes, on December 16th—Tesla rolled out a policy that addressed this issue by charging a fee ($0.40) for any additional minute the Teslas stay connected after being fully charged to incentivise people to return to their car and move it.

It's a simple solution to increase customer satisfaction and give everybody fair access to the Supercharger.

The choices, uses, and power of social media are almost endless, but whatever your final selection, it should make sense according to the business and marketing plans. Your efforts should all, along with the other steps of the Client Acquisition Blueprint, work towards the same goal—creating more value for more people in less time.

Get A *FREE* Video Deep-Dive Training here:
clientacquisitionblueprint.com/freegift
($297 Value, Yours *FREE*)

CONVERSION & AUTOMATION

Now that your foundation is set, and before you double down on driving traffic to your business, it's time to work on the next part of your Client Acquisition Blueprint: how to convert the traffic you're getting into quality prospects, and how to lead those prospects towards the decision of doing business with you.

Developing Irresistible Lead Generation Magnets and Creating Relevant Offers

With a solid foundation in place you'll undoubtedly be ahead of most of your competitors. You'll start attracting better clients and start dominating your market simply because people are able to find you and they can relate to you.

But what happens if your website is awesome, your brand is solid, and you know your Perfect Client Profile, but you're just not getting enough leads? Many people think they just need more traffic and people looking at their business. But before we jump into getting more attention and traffic to your website, the first step is to maximize the traffic you are getting. We do this by creating compelling reasons for these visitors to contact you, giving you their information so that they actually convert into a lead for your business.

Lead generation magnets are essentially free-of-charge resources and offers to persuade your Perfect Client to take the first step onto your Bridge and start the journey over to your side. This starts the process of:

1. Introducing prospects to your company, services and why you do things.

2. Pre-framing people so they know how to think about your business.

3. Educating them so you're working with people who 'get it' and are ready to take the next step—become a paying client.

Simply put: an irresistible free piece of highly relevant content that answers their most burning question, given to potential customers in exchange for their contact info (converting into a lead).

Sometimes people call this bait (imagine you're fishing, this would be the bait to capture the fish), freebies, free trials, samples (like at Costco), white paper reports, and so on.

We'll discuss some of the different types of lead magnets in this chapter, but in order to make your lead magnets work, you need to know what to offer your potential customers. What is it that they really want, and what do you have that will inevitably improve their lives and move them towards a decision of exchanging their money for your products or services? Only with relevant, easy-to-consume content will your lead magnet get the job done and get you their contact information. Once you have this, you can start the follow up process to convert them into paying customers.

What To Offer In A Lead Magnet

In Chapter 1 we discussed the Value Ladder concept. Look back at it and make sure you completed your value ladder. For our web department at my digital marketing agency, Just Digital, one of the lead magnets we offer is a website optimization checklist called: 7 Secrets to Getting More Leads from Your Website. It's something we get asked often, and it's a simple checklist we follow to make sure we're converting website traffic into leads.

Another thing we often get asked is, "How much is your web design?" We don't shy away from quoting prices up front because we know 80% of the people aren't right for us and we don't want to go through a whole sales process only to find out they can't afford us or they don't really know us. So at one point we had a Web Design Pricing download page promising an instant quote. Since most of our web design projects fell within three ranges depending on complexity, we were comfortable quoting them specific packages and ranges for the project up front, and the highest option has a bigger range that leaves us enough room for bigger, more complex projects. Once they downloaded the pricing sheet, we prompted them to schedule a call. Most people scheduled a call and talked to our team without even reading the pricing sheet. We generated a lot of new clients this way, simply by removing that question from our prospects' minds. We get enough lead flow that I'm ok with not working with the 80% of prospects that are shopping based on price and see a website or digital marketing as a commodity.

For our other services, quoting prices up front might not make sense, so we offer other lead magnets. In the case of web design, we decided we wanted to shift from selling just websites to selling complete digital marketing solutions. We still do web design, but the process of working with us has evolved and changed, and so have our lead magnets.

The content you offer in the lead magnet doesn't need to be complex or extensive, it simply needs to do two things:

1. **Add value to your potential customers by giving them something they want.** Ask yourself, what's the number one thing my clients want? Give them that up front.

2. **Opt-in**—Collect their contact information in exchange for the value you provide. The extent of the information you collect depends on the traffic source and how much trust you've previously established with your potential customer. It can be:
   a. Email Only
   b. Name and Email
   c. Name, Email, Phone Number
   d. In the case of the Web Design Pricing sheet, we

asked for a lot because if we were going to give away that much information up front, we wanted to make sure people were serious. So we asked for first and last name, company name, phone number, their role in the company, website URL, their industry, when they wanted to launch, plus any more details they wanted us to know. Surprisingly, people filled this out with accurate information.

When people pay you, they don't always pay you with money. They pay you with attention when they read, watch, or listen to your free content. They pay you with their trust, permission, and contact information when they opt in.

At this point, you've gotten something much more valuable than money: their trust and attention. Deliver value in the lead magnet and during your follow up, and you'll eventually earn their trust enough for them to give you money. Depending on what you're selling, you can now make an offer for them to buy something.

Types Of Lead Magnets

When thinking about what content type would work best for your lead magnet, think about your target audience. Do they enjoy reading or do they prefer videos? Do they want a simple answer or the whole backstory that gives them enough information on the why of your suggested solution? Once you answer these questions, you can select the best type. The most known and used ones are the following, but please don't feel like you should limit yourself to this list. What works for other companies might not work for you and vice-versa.

1. PDF Report
Providing advice and simple steps to follow for your client to get the result they want.

2. Cheat Sheets, Checklists
These are my favorite because they're almost immediately consumable and they provide specific results for people. A client

of ours is in the tax resolution industry (helping people with IRS problems) and he has a checklist titled: 9 Secrets To Getting IRS Penalties Removed that helps people avoid paying the insane penalties that the IRS imposes on unpaid taxes. A mortgage broker or real estate agent might use something like: 3 Simple Steps to Owning Your First Home, Even if You Don't Have Credit or Money Down in an effort to get more leads of first time home buyers.

3. Swipe Files or Templates

These are things your prospects can just fill in the blanks or copy. In my entrepreneurship and success program, Design An Epic Future, I help youth particularly in minority communities design a compelling future for themselves and create businesses around the problems they want to solve. I give people an editable version of my personal vision board to help them get started.

4, Whitepaper

Usually a longer research paper, or a solution you implemented, with all the steps and details that led you to the final result.

5. Case Studies

People are intrigued by case studies because they illustrate specific solutions and results for specific cases. What was the initial issue? How did you approach it? What did you do differently? What were the final outcomes?

6. eBooks

Sharing your expertise in more detail with examples, ideas, advice, and how-tos. Books can also fall into the category of lead magnet (including this book you're reading now).

7. Training Videos

Sometimes people don't really feel like reading, but wouldn't mind watching a short video. It's an especially useful tool to explain complex concepts or address issues that require a more personal approach.

8. Webinars or Live Workshops

These are longer training sessions on your subject. They usually last 45 minutes to two hours, but in some cases we've done webinars as long as four hours.

9. Free Consultations

Before the internet, this worked great because all the information was gated and only the experts had access to it. Now, this is the most common but also the least effective unless you've positioned yourself correctly and have efficient intake systems. In a consultation, there's no perceived value, so you have to really set up the value correctly before you give away your time.

10. Free Trials

Particularly common in software companies, but this is great for product companies and service companies alike. If you give away a $10 product but get a customer for life, the numbers make sense.

Which Type of Lead Magnet to Chose

I always recommend having a combination of lead magnets. For example, we offer a free webinar teaching the Client Acquisition Blueprint, but we also give them free training videos, free checklists, and even free swipe files. To check it out, go to clientacquisitionblueprint.com/freegift.

Yet, regardless of the type of content you feel comfortable creating, it should be created with a few key details in mind:

1. **It should do its best to fill a gap of knowledge** your leads have, so they can learn from it and improve their own lives.

2. **It should also provide solutions to any issues** they might have in a simple and straightforward manner. Instant gratification is a must in today's fast-paced world, so you should go straight to the point and deliver the value you promised.

If you feel your lead magnet is something you could actually charge money for, that's a sign that your lead magnet is going to be effective. Chances are your prospect can find that information online with a bit of research, but the goal is for you to distill that and synthesize it for them, saving your prospect hours of endless research.

By showing that you're willing to help your potential clients, you can start building a relationship that can prove to be very fruitful for you in the long run and even increase the lifetime value of your customers.

Even though lead magnets are great on their own, and it's perfectly ok to simply thank the visitor after they download your material, what is an even better approach is to wrap up with an offer. Quite simply, after the customer downloads the lead magnet, instead of getting to the usual "thank you" page, they get to a small offer page. Some marketers will call this an upsell, one time offer, or a tripwire. It's simply the next natural progression of the sales process. What do you want them to do next?

It doesn't need to be anything huge. It can include a call to action to book a call, schedule a free consultation, download a free version of the software you're working on, or whatever might open the conversation with the person and help you start building a relationship. It can also be a paid offer.

For a dentist, the lead magnet might be: 5 Simple, Organic Home Hacks to a Better, Brighter Smile for under $20, teaching people how to keep their smile healthy, and the small offer can be to come in for a free teeth cleaning, or $50 whitening kits. The goal of this is to get them into the office where you can then ascend them up the value ladder.

There's a very simple reason why this works. You're giving something up front of high perceived value they didn't have access to before, in exchange for something really small. For the cost of their name and email, they're getting immediate value that can help them solve an issue they're facing or improve their lives.

The important thing to take into consideration is the order. If you try to get people to commit to something in any shape or form, it won't work unless you're committing to an equivalent thing yourself. You have to commit to serving them first, then deliver on that promise.

That's why having people schedule a call or a consultation won't be as effective if the invitation appears before they get access to the lead magnet. If you move your consultation or paid offer after your lead magnet, your prospect will feel like they already got something from you that will help them live better, and that might just be the push many of them need to get in touch.

But, again, all of this won't work if you don't figure out what your Perfect Client wants and you present it to them in a way that stays true to your strategy, is authentic, uses a tone that resonates with the intended audience, and gives them instant value.

In the case of a dentist, there are different reasons why a patient would consider searching for information about a dentist. One might be that the person has a lot of pain and is in need of immediate relief from the pain they're experiencing. Another might be related to cosmetic reasons—they might be considering braces or Invisalign. The buying behavior for both of them is radically different. One wants to see the doctor and cares about hours of operation, reputation, and availability. The other cares about having all the information and doing research before making a decision. The lead magnets and offers should be adjusted to each context so it makes sense for the patient.

Conversion Pages

CHAPTER 7

"The Gateway to Profits."

How easy is it for people to give you money? Do you have effective pages where you can convert a visitor into a lead, and a lead into a client?

A conversion page, simply stated, is a stand alone web page that your visitors 'land' on, whose sole purpose is to convert that visitor into a lead or a lead into a client. This idea seems simple enough or maybe a bit broad: shouldn't all your web pages convert visitors into leads? While that may be your goal, that's usually not the case. You'll get 80% of your leads from only 20% of your web pages. These are what we call your Conversion Pages, though they're sometimes referred to as landing pages or by their different uses (opt-in pages, sales pages, registration pages, squeeze pages, etc).

In this chapter we'll discuss the different types of conversion pages, what goes on them, and where to use them in your marketing. It's important to realize and take note of where your traffic is coming from, what the flow of that traffic is, and what pages they are landing on first and last so you can make sure you're delivering the best possible marketing experience.

For example, a visitor Googles "transmission repair near me" and clicks on the first mechanic's website that pops up. However, they're taken to the services page that lists brake replacement or a variety of other services, so chances are this visitor won't take the time to glance through everything because it's not relevant to their specific need. If they can't find what they're looking for, what's most likely to happen is that they "bounce" and go to that mechanic's competitor who has a website with a more relevant conversion page.

Whenever there is an offer you want to propose to your leads, a well-designed conversion page is a game changer. It's basically a dedicated page focusing only on whatever it is you have to offer, the benefits of the product or service you're offering, and what your visitor needs to do in order to get that offer (a.k.a. the Call to Action).

What you offer on your conversion page might be free—your lead magnet for download (or paid) a low-level product or service to upsell to the customers based on your value ladder. This could happen either on the "thank you" page after they opted to receive your lead magnet, or later, when the communication exchange begins. Regardless of what you are offering, the conversion page should always have a clearly stated Call to Action (buy now, download now, get instant access, etc).

Your visitors should immediately understand what they are required to do when they land on your page. The content should relate only to this specific marketing task at hand—there's no need for generic content, banners, or excessive text customers should scroll through unless that text is persuasive copy.

The conversion page should be consistent with your brand, using the brand colors and images, and in the end, conveying the same message. Though it can also be adapted to the branding of the specific campaign you are promoting and the copy you use, it should drive people to take action. Don't sugarcoat the message. By keeping things highly relevant but simple and to the point, you have a better chance of convincing your potential customer and motivating them to take action.

The Four Main Types Of Conversion And Landing Pages

Depending on the traffic source and the marketing campaign you're running, this is where you'd place your lead magnets and offer them to your potential customers. But, not all conversion pages are the same. Yes, usually the two ultimate goals are lead conversion and sales conversion (which, let's be honest, are always the goal, even if the main purpose of the conversion page is to just provide useful information or educate the visitor). There are different types of conversion pages, each with its own specific purpose and goal:

1. Opt-in pages

These are the pages you'd put your lead magnets on. They are where you offer something of value, and in order to obtain it, visitors need to provide their contact information. By offering something relevant to the visitor, you'll be given their attention in return (remember, not all exchanges involve money!), as well as the opportunity to reach out to them and try to move them up your value ladder. These pages are responsible for about 80% of your lead generation. They can also be your registration pages, request a consultation pages, and any other free lead magnet we discussed in the Lead Magnets chapter.

2. Sales pages

These are your money making pages. They're the conversion pages that sell your product or service with a direct and strong call to action to convince the customers to spend their money right then and there. These can be long form sales letters with a buy button, sales videos, or simple product pages like you'd find in ecommerce or online stores. When it comes to offers, it can be anything from a discount offer (like a coupon, for example) to main product offers or order forms.

A note to service businesses: every business absolutely needs sales pages. Even if you're in services and you need to go through a longer sales process, you MUST have an easy way for people to give you money. If you need to have a contract signed first, then add a link in your contract to input payment information and send them to an order form. Even if the amounts are custom for every transaction, have them give you a fixed payment. It's about streamlining the sales process and creating frictionless transactions. Don't wait for prospects to call you or mail you a check.

Have the option for them to pay online. If you don't have a sales page and a way for people to give you money fast, then you literally have holes in your pocket. There are ways to apply for loans online, and without a doubt, people will be able to buy homes and cars online as well. Trust me. It'll happen. So please don't say, "This doesn't work for my business," because if you don't find a way to do it, someone else will.

3. Informational

As the name implies, the main goal of these landing pages are to provide relevant content on whatever subject your customers are seeking information on. These pages can be your homepage, about, or individual services page. These are essential for your foundation, SEO, and building trust and credibility. They will most likely bring in some of your organic traffic, but, generally speaking, these are not the conversion pages that bring in leads or sales.

Informational pages provide specific, technical information on whatever service or product you're dedicating the page to and it's likely that after reading this information, they'll want to get in touch with your company. This is where you send them to an opt-in page or maybe a sales page.

4. Educational and Utility Pages

Blogs
These blog posts should always have relevant calls to action at the end. The goal is to educate the prospect, then send them to an

opt-in page or sales page. By correctly using educational conversion pages, you'll nurture and build trust with potential customers. These will also drive the bulk of your organic traffic.

Utility Pages

These are simply where you might deliver the thing they asked for, such as the download page or even the thank you page. This is a great tool to keep momentum going and ask the visitor to take a small specific action, such as looking for the email you just sent, providing product delivery information, or if you just sold something, you might have an onboarding video to welcome the new client. These pages are essential to a great customer experience so people don't feel lost after they opt in or buy something from you.

Content Delivery Pages

If you're doing a free video series or delivering any piece of content, these pages simply deliver the content you promised. But they're also essential in progressing the sales conversation.

Aside from the informational pages, now you can understand why you shouldn't really see a conversion page as a mini version of your website. It's much more specific and targeted, and it has a unique purpose.

Since a landing page is technically any page that your visitor lands on, we're going to focus on only the two true conversion pages: opt-in pages and sales pages. These are the two types of pages that are either converting visitors into leads or converting leads into clients. So, what should your basic checklist be when working on your conversion page?

Three Elements Of A High Converting Page

1. Have a compelling and irresistible offer.

This cannot be stressed enough. The visitors that land on your conversion page (more often than not) don't want to know about when your company was established and what your team members like to do in their spare time. They have an itch they can't scratch, and they need to find a clear and attractive solution within the first few seconds on the page.

2. Great copy that turns words into action (ultimately money).

Humans are selfish by nature and we're always asking, "What's in it for me?" Answer that up front in your titles, headlines and calls to action. High quality sales copy is a game changer and an absolute must on a conversion page. Depending on the situation, people don't really want to read for hours on how to solve their situation, but would rather get to the point fast. Or, if their issue is very complex, they need to get a clear indication that they're on the right track early on. Good copy will help you retain the visitor on your landing page and convince them to do whatever your conversion page is asking them to do. Every copywriter has their own personal style, but here are the top copywriting formulas that convert:

1. **Motivated by pain**. We're more motivated by pain and the desire to resolve that pain than we are by anything else. Copy that emphasizes the prospects' pain will urge customers to take action immediately. When you're structuring your message for a conversion page, here's the basic copywriting formula:

   a. **Problem: Identify the problem**, call it out in the clearest terms, and tie the visitor into it, sometimes by calling them out directly. If you're in health and wellness, you might say something like, "Are you tired of being sick and tired? Are you tired of crashing at 4pm and having zero energy to spend time with your kids and family?"

   b. **Agitate**: Aggravate the problem even more. What will happen if they don't take action? Will the pain intensify and get worse? Take them through a mental journey and help them see what will happen if they don't resolve their issue.

   c. **Solution**: Offer your solution to their problem and help them solve their pain. This process might feel a bit negative or uncomfortable sometimes, but it's usually the type of copy that gets the best results. All you're doing in this process is highlighting the pain they already have in an effort to genuinely help them. There are some other elements you can add to this formula like leveraging testimonials, juxta positioning price and other options, and a few other more advanced techniques that can make this formula foolproof.

2. **Motivated by dreams and aspirations**. This naturally tends to have a more positive tone. It calls out what the reader desires and guides them through a journey of how they can achieve it. A good copywriting formula for this is known as the AIDA model—Attention, Interest, Desire, Action. It first seeks to draw attention (something different, exciting, bold) and spark interest, which then turns into a desire and results in a strong call to action. This formula can be applied across industries but it works especially well with luxury or non-essential items.

The Ultimate Sales Letter by Dan Kennedy and *How to Write Copy That Sells* by Ray Edwards are great places to start learning effective copywriting. Once you have your irresistible offer and great copy in place, you want to make sure you're not unintentionally giving people the opportunity to leave your page before they take action.

3. Distraction free.

When designing your conversion page, you should avoid overwhelming visitors—don't include additional information that doesn't directly tie into the problem they are looking to solve. That also means removing any unnecessary navigation, menu links, headers and footers.

1. **Only vital information**. It goes hand in hand with all the previous points of this list. Don't distract your visitors—give them what they came for, have them take one specific action, and that's it.

2. **Direct call to action.** Don't try to sugarcoat it—there's no need for that. There's a very specific value you're offering your customers and there's no point in not being direct about it. Are you asking them to download something? Fill out a form? Share? Call you? Pick one call to action and make it clear, make it obvious, be direct.

For a **FREE 14-day trial** with Clickfunnels, go to:
clientacquisitionblueprint.com/clickfunnels

What Software Should You Build Your Landing Page With?

Earlier I said that you shouldn't think of your conversion pages as a mini version of your website, so there must be a different way to go about building it tech-wise, right? Well, yes and no.

It is, in the end, a web page and you can go about it the same way you would with a website. But there is software which was made for the sole purpose of giving people all the tools they need to build a conversion page in a few minutes.

Here are the most commonly used options today:

1. Clickfunnels

I personally love this software and recommend it to everyone. They're built around the concept of Sales Funnels: a series of conversion pages, offers, and order forms that tie together to create a complete conversion page setup. For its monthly fee it offers a lot of options, such as basic landing pages, opt-in pages, sales pages, order forms, split testing, measures conversion rates, and comes with built-in automation capabilities. And it can integrate with WordPress via a plugin.

2. WordPress

We've talked about WordPress in detail in Chapter 3. All I'll say here is to follow the Three Elements of a High Converting Page we discussed above. Remove the standard header elements, navigation, and anything that might distract from your offer and call to action. Wordpress is highly customizable and you can find the mix and match of plugins that work best for you.

3. Leadpages

Great for landing pages and opt-in pages, and it can be integrated with WordPress as well. It works as a drag-and-drop, fill in the blank platform, so it's extremely easy to use. All you need are the elements you'd like to include and some time to play around until you get the result you're looking for. It also measures conversion rates. Instapage and Unbounce are a couple other options and do pretty much the same thing.

Putting It All Together:
Your Conversion Pages, Lead Magnets,
Offers And Measuring Success.

When it comes to actually building your conversion page, it's advisable to find somebody who already knows how to do it (you can start by checking with the freelancer or agency that worked on your website) and guide them through exactly what you want. Keep in mind most web designers and graphic designers aren't marketers, even if they're an agency or call themselves a marketing company. Make sure they have proven results and you're measuring key metrics for your conversion pages. We'll cover a lot of these metrics in the Paid Advertising chapter (Chapter 10).

A conversion page is a vital part of turning your website into an asset that generates real results for your business and real dollars in your bank account. It's the best way to monetize your online presence so getting it right is crucial.

The potential customer should have only two options: take action or leave. If they take action, they should keep moving across your Bridge to ultimately get to the side where you're at. If they leave, there's always the possibility of a retargeting campaign to drive them back to that same offer before moving on to another offer that might be more relevant to them (we'll also cover retargeting in the advertising section).

Many companies struggle with their sales processes, making them long and tedious for their customers, but with a simple conversion page and a relevant offer you can make the process quicker than you could ever imagine. What once took weeks, now takes just a few clicks.

Conversion pages allow you to streamline your sales process. It makes it much easier for customers to give you money because people visit pages in a sequential manner, giving you full control of your marketing message and sales process, much like you would in a one-on-one sales presentation.

Here's what your conversion page flow might look like, laid out visually.

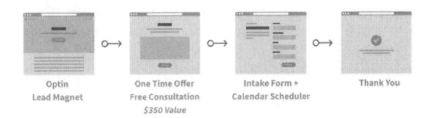

The elements (lead magnet, one time offer, etc) can change to match your business, but this is a simple conversion funnel that we've implemented for several service businesses like plastic surgery centers, chiropractors, dentists, interior designers, accountants, and law firms.

If you're able to sell something directly, you can do something like this:

As we'll cover in the next chapter, as long as you capture their email or contact information during the first step, you can now start the follow up process. Even better if that process is automated.

Measuring Your Conversion Pages

At the end of the day, we're after results. The better you understand your Perfect Client's needs, wants, and desires, the better your lead magnets and offers will become. The better your offers are, the higher your conversion rates on the conversion pages will be, both in terms of converting visitors into leads, and leads into clients. Coming up with great offers and testing different versions of the pages can be challenging, but it's worth the time and energy. For a small business or startup, it's important that you focus on results.

Get A **FREE Video Deep-Dive Training** and See Real Examples of Our Top Converting Pages Here: **clientacquisitionblueprint.com/freegift**

Automation: Marketing, Sales and Operations

CHAPTER 8

How to build an asset online that serves as the foundation for your online marketing.

With all the elements to consider when creating your marketing plan, things can quickly become overwhelming. Activities can take hours to complete, interrupting your schedule to post the next piece of content or respond to the emails and messages you receive. Wouldn't it be amazing if there was a way to make it all... simpler and more manageable?

Automation Allows You To Scale Your Business

Imagine this for a moment.

You wake up tomorrow, reach over to grab your phone, open up Facebook, and see that every major network is now promoting your business and promoting you as a celebrity in your industry.

Then you turn on the TV and see you're on the news. Every major media outlet wants an interview. Potential clients are knocking down your door wanting to talk to you, they're leaving voicemails and sending emails like never before.

What would happen to your business? Would you be able to handle that kind of extreme influx of leads to your business? Would you be able to fulfill and deliver at a high level? Would you be able to convert the thousands or tens of thousands of leads coming in every week?

The simple question is: *If every major media network, platform, or influencer promoted your business tomorrow, could you handle the business?*

This is a question I often pose to small business owners because it forces them to think of their businesses in a radically different way. Many times they've never really thought of scaling their business to that degree, and as a result, they haven't documented their processes nor created the systems that allow them to scale.

This is also true for marketing and sales. I can't tell you how many times I've worked with small business owners and we started generating leads, only to find their follow up with those leads was terrible or nonexistent. They get a phone call from a potential client, they jot down their info on a sticky note or lunch napkin, and forget to do anything with it because they're too busy putting out fires in their day to day business.

That's when automation comes in. We briefly covered it towards the end of the previous chapter, mentioning that conversion pages can help automate the sales process. Automation is essentially using software that helps schedule emails, send automatic replies when customers reach out, schedule posts across social media, help track the lifecycle of customers in your marketing, and process payments. This software can also aid in your product/service delivery, workflow automation, assigning tasks to people, and much more. By using automation, you can tackle all of your marketing and business tasks in a more efficient and effective manner, never letting things fall through the cracks again.

Deliver More Value, To More People, In Less Time

To really understand the role and value of automation, be it for your marketing, sales, or operations processes, let's take a quick look back to the role of the entrepreneur. If you recall from the beginning of the book, I said that an entrepreneur's role is to:

THE ROLE OF AN ENTREPRENEUR

1. Create value
2. Communicate that value
3. Exchange value (effectively and efficiently)

Your job is to figure out how to deliver more value, to more people, in less time.

You shouldn't have to write every reply to every email you get from scratch (or, if you're really organized, copy/paste from your templates).

With automation, you can get a lot of the mundane tasks done that might get in the way, as the name implies, automatically. You just need to take a bit of time to make sure it's all working properly in the beginning, then do periodic checkups and improvements.

Automation, from the perspective of the role of the entrepreneur, helps you tackle multiple tasks at a time by always running in the background, making sure you don't get distracted.

Thinking back to the question I posed earlier: what would happen if every major media company decided to promote your business tomorrow? Automation gives you the advantage of being able to handle the traffic and lead flow once you reach that level. You might think that you don't really need it now because you can easily handle everything yourself but now is actually the perfect moment to set everything up, because you have time to find the best mix of automation tools.

This way, when your business explodes and you're suddenly handling more clients than you ever anticipated, you already have everything in place, and can continue focusing on what matters most in a given moment.

Engage Your Perfect Client and Filter Out Those That Aren't

Another great benefit of automation is that it will help you filter people out. Many people send emails, call you, send out messages, or fill out a contact form but are not really serious about trying to find a solution or doing business with you.

As your business grows and your demand increases, you might have to be more selective with who you work with and only work with the people that allow you to do your best work, your Perfect Client Profile.

With automation, you can have people go through your process, ask them the necessary questions, send them materials, etc, and you're in the driver's seat. You're not bending over backwards for a cheap prospect who doesn't appreciate you, doesn't know you, and doesn't care about the value you deliver. You decide who should be your main focus and who should not based on their engagement and behaviors.

With an automatic sequence in place for people to go through, they'll be educated about your service to a point where they can decide whether or not they'd like to proceed. And the best part is that you didn't have to spend hours working with each customer to educate them in order to filter out those who don't make sense for you to work with.

Automating Your Sales Process

This is where your marketing efforts turn into sales efforts. The simplest and most seamless way to go about it is with an email sequence that delivers value to your prospect, educates them, leverages past results and testimonials, and drives them to the next step of your sales process (consultation, sales page, etc).

A conversion page, though not strictly automation, can also be considered a part of the automation process. Those who land on your conversion page do go through a set sequence of steps from clicking on the call to action. You're leading them through an automated funnel.

This sounds great, but how does it look in practice?

Automation In Practice

A client of ours, Dr. Gorgas, is a Functional Medicine doctor. A chiropractor by education, he's dedicated his life to alternative medicine and has a deep passion for helping patients reach optimal health and live a vibrant life. While traditional medicine focuses on eliminating diseases or simply maintaining them, functional medicine focuses on optimal functioning of the body and its organs, usually involving systems of holistic or alternative medicine.

One of Dr. Gorgas' practice areas is treating women with thyroid problems. His lead magnet on his conversion page is titled, "4 critical questions to ask when being rushed out of your doctor's office with new thyroid meds but you're still feeling lousy." When his potential patients hear him speak, watch a video of him, or get referred to him, they land on his website and they can download the report in exchange for their contact information.

Once the contact information is in the database, they enter into a 12-month-long automation sequence of follow-ups, during which they receive emails addressing any possible resistance they may have, answering their questions, presenting testimonials, offering additional information, and each email always includes the possibility of scheduling an appointment with him.

Over the span of 12 months, they'll receive 26+ pieces of communication from his office, all without him lifting a finger. In addition to the organic traffic generating efforts, he runs $30 a day in paid advertising on Facebook. The results: five to ten new patients every single month with a lifetime value in the thousands of dollars.

Case Study: $400,000 in 4 days

Another one of our clients, Michael Rozbruch, has a consulting business where he teaches CPAs, IRS Enrolled Agents, and attorneys how to help people with IRS problems. After building his own tax resolution firm to $23 million in annual revenue, he exited his company and started a brand new business consulting other practitioners and teaching them how to grow their tax practices. He puts on nationwide conferences, does consulting, and offers a comprehensive training program people buy for $2500.

We've been able to help him grow his new business in three years to almost $3 million in sales, through automation. I want you to start seeing everything come together: lead magnets, offers, and conversion pages, and I'll share with you a campaign that generated over $500,000 in sales during a five day period.

During a product launch we ran for Michael, we were able to generate $402,693 in sales during the four day launch window, plus get an extra $100k+ from the same customers after the initial purchase. About half of that came during a live webinar he did, the rest came through automated follow up emails after the webinar.

Ignore for a minute the questions of what product he sold or the specific industry, because after this example, I'll share how

Elon Musk used almost the exact process to launch a product he didn't even have ready to sell, yet was still able to get $14 billion worth of pre-orders for Tesla's Model 3.

So let's jump into the case study. Here's a breakdown of the results and the process we used for our client's $400k product launch:

1. **Webinar**: People registered for a four hour live online training session where he taught some concepts, interviewed past successful clients, and showcased his product.
   a. 3000 people registered to attend the presentation.
   b. 55.79% lead conversion—the percentage of people who registered (we had 5,778 visits to the page).

2. On the **thank you page**, the page they see right after they register with their name and email, we confirmed their registration and made a product offer for $197. We made this a **One-Time Offer**. Essentially this was a sale that they could only get on that specific page and once they left, they couldn't access it anymore. The offer included templates for sending out press releases and a training program on how to get free PR.
   a. 139 people bought the product at $197.
   b. Total Revenue from the one time offer: $27,383.
   c. 4.63% sales conversion—the percentage of people who purchased the one-time offer.

3. Automated follow up emails to remind people to show up.
   a. We had 11 emails go out before the event with four short training videos to keep people engaged and remind them of the event details. This was over the span of 21 days prior to the event. The frequency of communication automatically adjusted depending on what date the person signed up.

4. Webinar Broadcast.
   a. 36.43% show up rate. For webinars, people tend to register but then can't make it. A dropoff is

        expected here.

   b.   Number of Attendees: 1093 people actually showed up to watch the live presentation.

   c.   We sold over $270,000 during the first 90 minutes of the presentation.

   d.   Follow Up Emails: we sent another set of automated follow up emails for five days after the presentation that resulted in $402,693 in gross sales.

5.   Total Sales:

   a.   269 sales x $1497 product price = $402,693. We offered the product at a discount (from $2500 normal price) during the launch to incentivise people to buy.

   b.   Out of the 269 new customers, 107 of them subscribed to a $297 per month group coaching program. This resulted in an additional $31,779 per month in recurring revenue.

Tesla Case Study: $7.5 Billion in 24 hours, $14 billion in 7 days.

On March 31st, 2016 Elon Musk changed the game, again, for the auto industry. He unveiled Tesla's first electric vehicle aimed at the mass market, the Model 3. The previous three models were the Tesla Roadster (small production, exclusive, and priced at above $100,000) and the Tesla Model S (still a luxury car starting at around $60,000 and going up to over $100,000). The Model X is priced similarly to the Model S and aimed at the same high end market.

The Model 3 was poised to bring electric cars to the mass market priced at around $35,000. It was highly anticipated before the announcement, and it is undoubtedly a game-changing product, but the thing that fascinated me was Elon's launch strategy.

From the beginning, Tesla has taken a different sales approach with their direct-to-consumer sales strategy through their showrooms in malls and their website. This model changed the way people buy cars and bypasses the much dreaded car dealership shopping experience. People can go online and order their cars without having to deal with the haggling and ickiness that comes with buying a car.

With the Model 3, Tesla borrowed from a page in Apple's launch playbook: hype up the media (get organic traffic), invite people to a live event, and launch the product. With an unconventional and visionary leader like Elon Musk, the positioning was set, the raving fans were primed, and the launch strategy was executed phenomenally.

The basic process:

Registration   Watch Live   Order

The result:

Elon Musk ✓
@elonmusk   ⬫ Follow ⌄

Model 3 orders at 180,000 in 24 hours. Selling price w avg option mix prob $42k, so ~$7.5B in a day. Future of electric cars looking bright!

RETWEETS   LIKES
18,303   25,152

9:11 AM - 1 Apr 2016

↩ 951   ⬆ 18K   ⬒   ♥ 25K

There's obviously a lot of factors, work, and nuances that went into this product launch—like a revolutionary product, an unshakeable foundation, a solid strategy, a great brand, and remarkable leadership and vision that attracts people—but this is a model that works.

Their process was simple, but the execution was flawless. They invited people to the event, presented the product, and made it super easy for people to give them money with a simple order form online.

 **Elon Musk** ✓
@elonmusk   ❧+ **Follow**   ⌄

Over 325k cars or ~$14B in preorders in first week. Only 5% ordered max of two, suggesting low levels of speculation.

RETWEETS   LIKES
4,722   9,971

9:24 AM - 7 Apr 2016

↰ 690   ⇄ 4.7K   ≋   ♥ 10K

7 days after the Model 3 was announced, Tesla had over 325,000 Model 3 orders, resulting in about $14 billion in future revenue for the company, and over $350 million in cash from the $1000 deposits collected.

 For a video walkthrough of the case studies, visit:
clientacquisitionblueprint.com/freegift

A Record Day for Online Sales

On November 11, 2016, Alibaba (the Chinese ecommerce giant) broke the world record for most sales in a day. Singles day was an informal holiday for people not in a relationship, and in 2009, Alibaba turned it into a discount shopping day. In 2016, it recorded $17.8 billion in sales in that day alone.*

For comparison, Adobe Digital Insights reports that 2016's Cyber Monday hit a new record of $3.45 billion spent online.

Don't Let Your Small Business Limit Your Ambitions

At this point, you're either excited, extremely overwhelmed, or have completely dismissed this as a fantasy and you're sure this would never work for your business.

You may not see your small business as ever becoming a billion dollar company, but unless you step up your game and commit to building an epic business and creating a solid marketing strategy, your competition will swallow your market share. You started the business to do something that mattered, for yourself and for your customers. It may not be massive in scale, but if you believe in what you're doing, then you should have a system that can serve more people.

We tend to limit ourselves based on our current reality, based on what we think is possible for ourselves. So before you dismiss anything in this book, just give it a shot. The best thing I've ever done in marketing, business, and in life, is to test stuff. Just start, give it a shot, improve, then test again.

Alibaba Biggest Day
http://money.cnn.com/2016/11/10/technology/alibaba-singles-day-shopping-festival-breaks-records/

When I started out, I couldn't really grasp how people made money like this. I had a skewed perception of money due to the fact that I grew up with no money, and that everyone around me had no money.

When I started helping my family make money as a kid, I was used to going door to door, one by one, person to person and trying to make a buck. Scaling, automation, record sales days, and even marketing, were foreign concepts to me.

Even after starting my marketing agency, I spent the first few years of my career designing brands, building websites, posting on social media, and hoping this would create results for our clients and ourselves.

But I was missing this key piece: the conversion part of the Client Acquisition Blueprint. I had a solid foundation, but I wasn't getting any leads. Then I started getting more leads, but they weren't converting. I didn't have a clear offer, I didn't have an easy way for people to give us money, or I was too busy to give potential clients the proper attention they deserved. Not having automated systems resulted in a bad experience for people trying to do business with us.

I got tired of sending out complex proposals, endless pitch meetings, and having a limited capacity to serve only a handful of clients. So I decided I needed to implement this stuff into my own business. Once I figured out how to create irresistible offers, set up epic conversion pages, and create simple automation sequences in my business and in our clients' businesses, things started to really take off.

I acknowledge some of this might be a bit overwhelming, it may seem unreal, or confusing, but if you break it apart and implement it one step at a time, you'll start truly creating an asset that can help you scale your business.

The Different Types of Automation That Can Exponentially Increase Your Results

In the list below we'll cover the most common types of automation along with some simple examples of how to use automation to exponentially increase your sales, leads, and referrals. Automation can also decrease the amount of time, money, and energy you spend on certain tasks.

1. Marketing & Sales Emails

a. Indoctrinate

Introduce your company and yourself to prospects, guide them on how to think about your business, introduce them to your world views, walk them through The Bridge and get them to your side. These can be very simple emails with your basic information, social media links, information about your company, your why, and the value you offer. Sending quick videos or testimonials in these emails are also a great way to build trust and credibility.

b. Delivery of the promised lead magnets

Very often the lead magnets are not downloaded from the website but sent to the customer's email address. If you promise a report, a simple auto responder that delivers the lead magnet will ensure everybody gets what you've promised them. Setting up an email follow up sequence for the lead magnet, then moving them into other offers is crucial.

c. Phone call follow ups

A simple, "It was great chatting with you today!" email right after you talk to someone will make a great impression. Setting up an automatic reminder for you to call them back in three days will also ensure your important contacts aren't neglected.

d. Answer objections

It's human nature to have objections and wonder, "What if?" In your marketing and sales emails, you can address them one by one to convince customers to give your product or service a chance.

e. Deliver helpful information

Everybody wants to make an informed decision, so much more so if the decision is a big one. Offering additional information will help you build your credibility in the eyes of the customer, as well as work on a long-lasting relationship.

f. Tell stories

Nothing says quality and builds trust more than a genuine testimonial or case study. People enjoy hearing stories, especially inspirational ones that they can identify with, so leverage every happy client you can to broadcast their positive experience. Showcase their transformation and the before and after of their situation.

g. Offers

From your core products/services, discounts, and special offers to free consultations and upsells, you absolutely must make offers and invite prospects to do business with you. Sometimes all it takes is a little nudge. It may be exactly what they need to take that final step and agree to an exchange.

h. Onboarding emails, delivery emails

Welcoming people as clients, letting them know about the status of their delivery, etc. Existing customers are much more likely to buy from you again or buy more from you, and making offers right after they purchase is a great way to increase transaction value.

i. Tools to use

Affordable options for email marketing are Constant Contact, Aweber, and Mailchimp. They start at less than $50 and give you a nice suite of tools to create auto responder sequences, signup forms, and email list management. More robust options like Infusionsoft, HubSpot, Marketo, and Salesforce are the leaders in marketing automation and cost hundreds per month and can be thousands to set up. These options sometimes appear cumbersome to small business owners or unnecessary, but they're a worthwhile investment if you're serious about your business growth. They provide you with the infrastructure, support, and robust options your business needs to scale. Having an efficient business is priceless.

These are just simple examples to get you thinking of the types of communications you can start to automate. The key is to simply start and start simple. You can do so with a simple auto responder email sequence. Here's an example of how we would structure a two week automated follow up sequence using the above email types after someone downloads a lead magnet.

The FORTUNE is in the AUTOMATED follow-up.

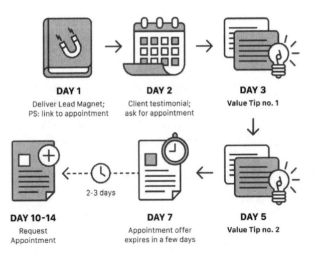

DAY 1
Deliver Lead Magnet;
PS: link to appointment

DAY 2
Client testimonial;
ask for appointment

DAY 3
Value Tip no. 1

DAY 10-14
Request
Appointment

2-3 days

DAY 7
Appointment offer
expires in a few days

DAY 5
Value Tip no. 2

We'd automate this flow using Infusionsoft.

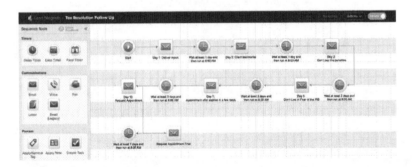

2. Social Media Scheduling

With tools like Buffer or Hootsuite you can schedule your social media content and postings. You can just spend an hour or two on a Tuesday morning to schedule a week's worth of posts, then not worry about having to post every couple of hours. When someone finds you on social, they'll be more likely to engage with you if your profiles don't look inactive.

Workflows

At Just Digital, most of us work remotely. Even our team in Los Angeles works remotely (if you've ever been stuck for two hours in 405 traffic, you'd want to work remotely as well—and pull your hair out). I like the freedom of it and so does our team. The only way I could run an efficient team is by automating things and having a solid system for managing our remote team.

When we get a new project, we automatically create tasks using a project management tool called Podio. We input the project type and it automatically generates a workflow, assigns tasks to the team, creates deadlines, and when a group of tasks are checked off, it triggers a new phase of the project and the project keeps moving forward. If anything falls behind, it notifies the project lead and reminds the person responsible. Of course, this still requires monitoring and human input, but it automates the thought process and ensures we're able to deliver a quality service to our clients.

Many small businesses don't have processes in place, they kind of "go with the flow," which might work for them now, but as the business grows, there's less and less time for improvisation.

Having set processes will help get the job done quicker without forgetting about any little details, and detailing these processes in the project management tool will help you and your team be more productive, effective and efficient when working, meaning you'll be able to service more customers and scale up when the time comes.

3. Prospecting and Sales

HubSpot, in addition to their marketing automation software, has a great sales and customer relationship manager software that helps track the sales process and helps salespeople be even more productive. It has quickly become a personal favorite of mine for its intuitive tools and ease of use. A couple of ways we way we use it at Just Digital are:

▷ **Finding potential leads**: The software pulls our prospects' company data such as revenue, phone number, employees, LinkedIn, Twitter, etc right on the contact dashboard. We don't have to scrape the internet, go to a company's contact and about pages to try to find the right person to talk to, or spend a bunch of time Googling people to find their social media accounts. It's all in one dashboard.

▷ **Dialing numbers**: There's an integrated service to call these leads. No more copy and pasting into Skype or trying to get it right when dialing on your office phone. Hit a button, the call happens, and a record appears so you have notes on what happened when.

▷ **Emailing**: It allows you to create a simple sequence of follow-up emails and it syncs with our Google Suite email. I can also schedule emails right from my Google email account and see if people open my emails, when they open them, and if I see they're engaged but haven't heard from them, then I can call right away while they're thinking about me.

▷ All records are seamlessly passed from my Google email to Hubspot so I don't have to even think about logging information.

▷ **Follow-up tasks**: You can create the follow-up tasks from there, which have notifications so you don't forget about anything.

▷ **Email templates**: You can save them and have them easily accessible, so you don't have to copy-paste from local folders on your computer.

▷ **Meeting scheduler**: With a scheduler tool that syncs and finds available times on our calendar, we avoid having to go back and forth to find a time that works for our prospects. Instead we send them a link to find a time that best works for them. Simple and painless.

This is partially automation but it's a bit more nimble and it allows the flexibility to change things on the fly if needed. The goal is to leverage tools and automation so our business can scale.

4. Calendar, Consultations Scheduling, and Appointment Booking

Salespeople, consultants, attorneys, spas, salons, medical practices, and everything in between need to schedule appointments or meetings on a consistent basis. With dedicated tools like ScheduleOnce, TimeTrade, Acuity, Square Appointments, etc you can streamline the process of setting appointments, making it easier for transactions to happen.

With these, there's no more going back and forth regarding the time slots that work best for everybody and sending invites once everybody agrees. It should take two clicks to schedule an appointment, not a five minute conversation.

5. Sending out contracts, proposals, and documents

If you're in services, you surely spend hours every month preparing proposals or quotes, sending agreements, waiting for your prospects to scan and send them back, waiting to get paid, then starting the work.

That's killing your sales and revenue. You can streamline all of that with tools like DocuSign and HelloSign. All of this can be done with a few clicks and an electronic signature. If the prospect doesn't sign, it reminds them until they do.

The Time and Money Invested Will Pay Off

It can all get very techy very quickly. If this is new for you, just bear in mind the time you'll get back as a result of spending a few hours on setting stuff up. This can magnify as your business scales.

If your assistant spends ten minutes doing a task (scheduling, searching for a file and emailing it, etc) and he does that task 20 times a week, that's 200 minutes a week, or 3.3 hours. Doesn't seem like much but in a 48 week year, that's 9,600 minutes or 160 hours. If you're paying him $3000 a month, that can be $3000 in savings to your business if you fully automate the task. If you simply cut the time it takes him to do that task from ten minutes to five minutes, that's saving $1,500. It's also time he can be doing higher value activities. This magnifies the more staff you have and the bigger your business gets.

Seems Like Automation is Just Email Marketing, But Isn't Email Dead?

No.

I wish I could leave it at that, but let me expand a bit because, though there are more types of automation that can be used, a lot of marketing automation is a more advanced form of email marketing.

People have the tendency to dismiss email as an outdated or ineffective communication method, especially with the advent of social media, messaging apps, and a widespread myth that younger generations simply don't use email.

Here are just three reasons why email is still the dominant form of communication.

1. An email list is an asset you control.

You don't really own your Facebook fan page, Instagram accounts, etc. If one platform dies out, like Vine or Myspace, you can't just pick up your fans and take them to another platform. If they change their rules and you lose half of your reach, it can be a fatal blow to your business. You can, however, take your email list and switch email softwares if you'd like. If your email marketing software disappears or changes their rules (as tends to happen with social media), you can simply take your stuff and move on without losing the most valuable thing your company has: its list of customers and prospects.

2. Reach + analytics.

Open rates on email are higher than the percentage of people who view your social media posts. If you have 2000 emails and 2000 fans, your email open rate can be around 20% compared to less than 10% on Facebook. Though some platforms have better reach in the beginning, inevitably as their user generated content explodes, their algorithms change to filter for the best content, thus dropping your reach. Some platforms simply have so much content that they can't possibly show everything to your audience.

3. Important stuff still happens on email.

Millennials still have to pay bills. Transaction records, receipts, purchase information, shipping information and other important correspondence still happens on email. Your customers expect it—even if they're younger and they swear by their favorite messaging app, they still pay bills using their email.

With an estimated 205 billion emails sent per day, the reality is that email is still the most universally used form of communication. Just think, how do you log in to Facebook? With email. Even to sign up for a social media account you need an email. So email is **definitely not dead**.

Where Should I Start?

1. Maximize what you already have.

There are countless shiny softwares out there that promise to solve all your problems. They don't. Chances are your business is already using some software for things like bookkeeping, contact management, etc. I always recommend to start there and maximize what you already have; chances are you're only using a small percentage of what the software can do. Also, having a folder of email templates, standard responses, and messages will help when it comes time to actually implement a robust marketing automation solution.

2. Map things out.

Before you start automating things or jumping into a new software, you'll need to take some time to map out everything that happens in your business. Just start listing things or draw boxes and start connecting them. From your marketing and sales processes to your operations and delivery processes, you need to get a full picture of what happens in your business. Then go deep on each category: what goes 1st, 2nd, 3rd?

A quick note on operations: I believe everything is marketing and everything contributes to the experience your clients have with you. Your operations are a part of your value creation process. Marketing is the communication of value, and you're communicating value with every touch point.

3. Commit to something.

When you decide to use a software, commit to using it 100% and go fast on implementing it. If it doesn't work, you'll find out faster. Don't get hung up on the technology, it's important but not important enough for you to pause your business and try ten different softwares. Find an IT consultant or business consultant with a bit of tech background to help you set your systems up. Whatever you do, just start and commit to using it.

Get A *FREE* Video Deep-Dive Training here:
clientacquisitionblueprint.com/freegift
($297 Value, Yours *FREE*)

GETTING MASSIVE ATTENTION

Now that your foundation is set, your conversion and automation is in place, it's time to work on the final part of your Client Acquisition Blueprint: how to get massive attention and exposure for your business. This is the fun part and it's an ongoing, never ending effort. As you'll learn in this final section, there are really only two ways to get attention: Organic and Paid.

Getting Organic Traffic & Expert Positioning

CHAPTER 9

Using content creation and distribution to create organic traffic, positioning, and thought leadership. How to go from chasing people and chasing business to having people come to you ready to buy.

Congratulations! We've now made it to the final two steps of your **Client Acquisition Blueprint** —*Getting Massive Attention*. These two chapters are probably the most important part of your digital marketing strategy—they're the fuel that makes everything run. It's what brings qualified people to your business and it's what gives you the opportunity to acquire clients.

This is also one of the biggest problem businesses have: they simply don't know how to get people's attention and their business lives in obscurity. Nobody knows they exist, or at least not enough people know they exist.

Without the ability to get attention you won't have the opportunities to convert visitors into leads and turn those leads into clients. Without the ability to generate interest in your business, you'll always struggle with cash-flow issues, you'll run on fumes and be scared to lose clients. You'll end up hanging on to bad clients you'd otherwise let go if you had a choice, just because you don't have any other choice nor do you have more opportunities coming in.

How to Cut Through The Noise

Marketing is the communication of value, but without people to communicate with, your fancy website and epic conversion pages don't matter. You need to get attention, massive attention. This also requires massive action, energy, patience, testing, and just raw persistence.

The market is noisy and because of how easy it is to start a Youtube channel or stream your message on Facebook Live, more and more people are doing it but few are actually succeeding and getting real results. In these next two chapters we'll cover how to cut through the noise with the right strategies and tactics, but it'll be impossible to cut through the noise unless you believe in your product 100%. If you're not absolutely sold on your product or service, why should your prospects be?

You need to come from a place of duty and responsibility to serve your clients better than anyone else. People need what you have. It's your job to do whatever it takes to get their attention and help them. Think of yourself as having the cure for cancer, or a life saving remedy. If you deeply believe in your value, you'll find a way to get their attention. If you don't, your competitors will sell them an inferior product and not truly solve their problem.

The Marketing Secret Formula: A Shortcut To Results

Some people are tempted to start with getting attention and more traffic to their websites. Those that do so without first implementing the last eight steps in the Client Acquisition Blueprint usually end up spinning their wheels and burning out. Getting attention for your business can be exhausting and expensive, especially without the proper systems to turn the attention into action and dollars in your bank account.

If you want fast results while you're building the rest of your Client Acquisition Blueprint, the reality is you can start with a very simple campaign that consists of just three steps:

1. **Create an irresistible offer** that your clients want, not that you think they want. There's a huge difference.

2. Set up your **conversion pages** that:
   a.   Collect leads
   b.   Sell something

3. **Get Attention**: Use one of the two ways of generating traffic to your conversion page. We'll cover these two ways in these two chapters.

Though the process is simple, the execution is not easy and requires the tedious work of testing and optimizing. Once you have these three things running, keep optimizing steps 1 and 2, and get creative with how you get attention. Test and optimize. That's the entire game.

A word of caution with "shortcuts"

Some people find great results with this formula. They make loads of money with one traffic technique, one landing page, or one offer, and they make the mistake of thinking that that's what marketing and business is all about. When you find someone selling you a "secret marketing formula," it's usually a prepackaged campaign that worked well for your industry. It can range from SEO to Facebook Ads and auto responder sequences.

It's a mistake to just use this shortcut because, as with most shortcuts, it's not the entire journey. You still have a long way to go towards building a well-rounded marketing plan. You can't succeed in the long run without a solid and foundational understanding of marketing. That's what the Client Acquisition Blueprint is meant to help you with. It's a complete, holistic, well-rounded approach to building a sustainable business.

By all means, use shortcuts—they're like chocolate or coffee. They have great short term effects, they're very yummy, but unfortunately you can't live off of them. So don't substitute shortcuts for your Client Acquisition Blueprint.

The Only Two Ways Of Getting Attention

When I say there are only two ways, I mean that every traffic generating strategy fits in these two categories: the organic approach, which is what we'll go through in this chapter, and the paid approach, which we'll take a deeper dive into in Chapter 10. These two chapters are probably the most important part of the digital marketing strategy—they're the fuel that makes everything run. However, since they don't work without having the foundation and leads conversion in place, we saved it for last.

Organic traffic generating strategies are those that require mostly energy and creativity and you're not directly paying for any advertising. In traditional grassroots marketing, this would be like having someone dance outside your business with a sign, putting flyers around town, networking, referral marketing, or putting on events with a street team. Though you're still paying people (like the guy dancing outside with your sign) and you're still paying for materials (such as flyers, brochures, and tshirts), you're not paying an advertiser like you would with TV, radio, billboards, or direct mail.

In Chapter 5 we covered the different social media channels available today. In this chapter we'll cover what goes on these social media channels and how to use them to get attention and generate traffic for your business. The amazing thing about building an organic online presence is that it builds authority, positioning, influence, and has a long lasting effect on your market—something that is difficult to create by paying for advertising (unless you have really deep pockets).

Something to keep in mind when we're talking about generating traffic: we're ultimately sending traffic to your conversion pages where they can either become a lead for your business or buy something from you. This is the thing most marketers and business owners miss that hinders them from translating their influence into income.

Answering The Most Important Question with Content Marketing and Social Media

Being in all of the right places, using the correct social media, and having a beautiful website won't do much for you if you're not taking strategic action. You need high quality and relevant content that will support your message and connect with your existing or potential customers.

Content can be useful to promote your business, but if it's irrelevant, off strategy, or simply "regurgitated" content, it can do more damage than good. Your main focus should be getting people to know you, telling your story, taking a moment to say, 'Hi, this is the value I can bring to your life, this is who I am and why I'm doing this.' It's the equivalent of shaking hands and kissing babies, or networking and meeting people.

Make sure you're leading with how you can serve and the value you provide to your clients. When it comes down to it, your potential clients don't really want to know how awesome you are. They're thinking about themselves and they're looking to see how (and if) you can address their issues. They're subconsciously always asking, "Is this for me?" and, "What's in it for me?"

Think about what your customers want to learn: what knowledge do they lack, and how can you best communicate your expertise? How can you let them know you're the absolute best without sounding too pretentious, self-absorbed, and a know-it-all? These organic strategies help you do that because by nature, they allow you to genuinely help your clients up front.

How Kim Kardashian Motivated Me To Write This Book

Even the senseless Youtubers and celebrities are providing their own unique value by entertaining millions every month, creating a sense of community, and a model of what their fans aspire to become. I may not agree with that but I still respect the social media influencers and celebrities for their ability to connect with millions.

Kim Kardashian's estimated networth in 2016 was $51 million according to Forbes. She has no musical ability, acting ability, nor any objective skill set. So why is she so freaking rich?

Without turning this into a case study of how Kim Kardashian became Kim Kardashian, here's my answer: influence. It's a simple fact: the more people that know you, watch you, and listen to you, the more money you can make because you can transform that attention into action. Influence translates to income sooner or later.

One day after a long 16 hour work day, I locked the office, called an Uber, and headed down the elevator. I was tired, hungry, and sleepy, but I felt good because I was doing what my parents taught me would make me successful: working hard. While waiting for my ride to arrive, I opened Instagram and saw a Kim Kardashian post about the launch of her new mobile app. In 2015, she made $71.8 million from that game alone.

I honestly got pissed off at society. How can we reward her and value her that much? I felt I was providing real value to people and I'm not even a fraction as successful as that. Of course, it was a bit silly and unproductive to be upset. An entertainer and celebrity's success has nothing to do with my success.

So I made a commitment and became more motivated to increase my influence and expand my ability to help more businesses succeed beyond just the clients we can serve one-on-one at Just Digital.

One thing I've realized in the past five years of doing this full time is that getting people's attention is hard! Celebrities sing and dance for your attention. Comedians make fun of themselves for your laughs. Companies pay billions to annoy you with their advertisements and hopefully get a few seconds of your attention.

With so much noise and competition for attention, it's important to remember this: you don't need millions of followers to make your efforts powerful or worth your time. These strategies are a way for you to connect with real people. People that have real problems and desires. All you need is to genuinely connect with the right people and serve them the absolute best you can.

Top Strategies For Organic Traffic

These next five steps need to be scheduled and executed in an orchestrated manner. The first few months are just to get you comfortable with creating content and understanding the platforms. After that, you can start really working on increasing your reach and even enlist expert help to take your efforts to the next level.

Here are the five steps most of the organic traffic strategies require you to take:

1. Create and publish content.

2. Distribute and share your content.

3. Engage with people who have an interest in your content and build an audience.

4. Nurture your relationship with this audience.

5. Optimize for discoverability: adding keywords to your videos, optimizing your blog posts with standard search engine optimization practices and keyword rich content. We covered basic SEO in Chapter 3.

It doesn't take much to create content and broadcast it, so there's basically no excuse for not working on your content strategy. You need to take it seriously and invest the time necessary to end up with content that makes sense to your clients and establishes you as an authority. Now, make no mistake—this is a long term game. **_You won't see results overnight_**. But the results you'll see in the long run will blow your mind away!

Start with a three month view of actions, topics, and metrics you need to track. Create a content calendar with the subject, topic, media type, and distribution or posting schedule. If you're a dentist, your content calendar can look something like this:

1. Subject for first month: Aesthetic Dentistry
   a. Topic #1: Invisalign vs braces
      i. Media type: Video with transcription or written summary. Create an image with a quote for Instagram.
   b. Topic #2: Teeth whitening
      i. Media type: Blog post with links to your appointment page
      ii. Create an image with a quote for Instagram.
   c. Topic #3: Veneers
      i. Media type: Video with transcription or written summary. Create an image with a quote for Instagram.
   d. Topic #4: Celebrity dentistry makeovers
      i. Media type: Blog post with before and after pictures. Create an image with a quote for Instagram.

2. Posting Schedule:
   a. Monday: Post blog or video. Email your patients and potential patients.
   b. Monday and Friday: Share a direct social media link.
   c. Wednesday: Post Instagram quote.
   d. Daily: Using pieces of the article, post directly on Twitter and Facebook using a tool like Buffer or Hootsuite (like we covered in the automation chapter).
   e. Tuesday and Thursday: Go on Instagram Live or Facebook live to chat about the week's topic, expanding on it or reiterating what it talks about. It's a good place to spend a few minutes with your audience and answer any questions they might have.

Once you have the first month down, you can do the same for the other two months in the quarter. After three months you'll have a nice library of content and you'll get better at it. Just put stuff out there, that's the only way to improve. This same process can apply for any and every industry and subject.

If you have the time or enjoy this, you can do all of it yourself and it might take you 10-20 hours a month. Just make sure you're consistent. Some of our busy small business clients can create an entire month's worth of content using this formula in just under two hours a month. Then they pass it on to their marketing assistant to handle the editing, posting, and engagement.

Our bigger clients can hire a team to do this for them. From the research, writing, editing, and the person on camera representing their brand, they leverage other people to execute their content strategy. A common misconception is that organic traffic strategies are all free. They're not. They cost either time and energy, or hard earned dollars and an awesome team.

Types of Content You Can Produce and How To Build Expert Positioning

In our Client Acquisition Blueprint Online Masterclass we've created frameworks and templates for each content type. Once you produce your first pieces of content, it's important to develop a simple checklist or outline for producing it so it's easier and faster to do. Things like having a standard introduction line for your videos, introducing the topic, going into the tips, and ending with a call to action all speed up the process of producing consistent content.

Now that you have a framework for thinking about content production, here are some of the media types for you to consider.

1. Videos

These can be recorded or livestreamed on platforms like Facebook Live or Youtube Live. Don't let the technology stop you from recording video. Most smartphones have amazing cameras, and with a decent lavalier microphone from Amazon, you can get amazing production quality.

When you're just starting out, the length of the videos is usually not as important as consistency. You can produce videos that are a only few minutes long (2-5 minutes), medium length (TED Talks are around 18 minutes), or longer content (30 - 45 minutes) where you really go in depth on the topic. Micro videos—videos that are only a few seconds long like on Instagram and Snapchat—are also great. Find what works for you and just start.

2. Articles And Blogs

Establishing yourself as an authority requires some written content as well. Whether you enjoy writing or not, written articles are a must. If you don't enjoy writing or don't have the time, you can hire freelancers to interview you or research your subject, then write the articles for you.

You can turn your articles into videos or podcasts, or my favorite method is turning videos and podcasts into blog posts. Written text is powerful and is also the best for SEO. The most common places to post blogs is on your website, but you can get creative with blogging platforms like LinkedIn Pulse, Medium, Tumblr or Blogger.

3. Social Media Postings

Aside from a place to distribute content, this can be the most ambiguous and difficult to figure out for some people. Most platforms allow you to post text, images and videos, but the context is much more important. In Chapter 5 we covered the different reasons why people are on social media, the types of platforms available, and the nuances of each. It's the difference between a professional networking event and a local bar. Don't be that guy that gets kicked out of either.

An important thing to keep in mind with social media posts are that these need to help you connect with people. I can't stress this enough. Social media is meant to be, you know, social. Be authentic, real, insightful, transparent, witty, valuable, and let your personality show. People can tell when you're trying too hard and being inauthentic, just like in a bar or networking event.

4. Media Appearances

One of the most powerful tools is to appear in respected publications in your industry and mainstream media. People treat you differently if they know you've appeared on TV or were featured in Forbes, for example. It's one of the best ways to create instant celebrity and credibility. Of course, you get the massive added benefit of being exposed to thousands or even millions of people through their established audience. One of my good friends is a top litigation attorney in West LA and his entire marketing strategy is doing a daily 90 second radio interview. He jumps on, answers a quick question, and he's been doing that consistently for over ten years. When people want to talk to him in person, they pay a $500 fee for a short consultation. Not everyone is willing to pay it, but the ones that do are his best clients who trust, respect, and value his services.

5. Becoming an Author

Taking the time to write your own book on a matter which you'd like to be perceived as an expert is a very powerful tool in building expert positioning. Having published works gives you credibility and can open many doors that otherwise wouldn't be an option.

6. Podcasting

The Pew Research Center reports on journalism.org that in 2016, 21% of Americans listened to podcasts. That number has risen steadily every year. I personally love podcasts and audiobooks. Having your own podcast is a great way to build an arsenal of content and a loyal audience of listeners. Being interviewed on one that's already established is a great way to tap into a new audience.

7. Partnerships with Influencers

You can leverage your connections or find influencers and borrow their audience rather than create your own from scratch. Ask to add value to their audience with a piece of content, an interview, or free stuff.

Find ways to deliver value to the influencer first and earn an opportunity to promote your business to their audience in the future. Imagine getting a shout out from a celebrity. One connection or partnership can change your life.

Sometimes, just by association you can build celebrity and influence. Being the friend of a celebrity, authority, or influencer automatically positions you in a different category from the rest. Obviously build the relationships in a genuine way and create win-win situations.

8. Contributions To Communities

Sites like Quora and Reddit have strong communities of hyper engaged members where you can connect with people interested in your topic. Facebook groups and LinkedIn groups are also a great option. Starting your own groups is even better.

Often, people will ask questions and you can answer them, instantly building expert status. You'll find entire communities that are already searching for what you have to say. These will become some of your best sources of leads. A plastic surgeon client of ours saw a great increase in website traffic when he started answering questions on realself. com, a website where people go to discuss their plastic surgeries and ask questions.

These sites and communities are a great place to source content ideas as well. Ninja tip: reading your competitors' negative reviews on Yelp, Google+ or Amazon can help you understand weaknesses in your marketplace and your customers biggest pain points.

4 Quick and Easy Ways to Produce Content

Creating content doesn't have to be hard, but if you feel like you can't do it or it's not your strength, just try this simple exercise before we start.

Think of three pieces of advice you'd give people on each of these subjects:

▷ How to live a healthier life.
▷ How to have a great relationship (even if you're not currently in one).
▷ How to make more money or save more money.
▷ How to be a more moral or spiritual person.

Most people have advice to dispense in each of these subjects and can come up with three things for each in less than five minutes. Even a college kid can give you relationship advice! If you're an expert in your industry, don't take your knowledge and years of experience for granted. Even if you think the stuff you know is common knowledge or it's only a quick Google search away, to your audience it may be new and it may also help them to hear it from a different voice and perspective.

If you're not quite sure where to begin when coming up with content ideas, here are four quick and easy ways to get started:

1. The Top Ten

Take the top ten things you want your potential clients to know and create content around those, either as blog posts or short videos.

2. Turn Questions into Content

Surely you're often asked questions about your business and the value you offer. Whenever that happens, take it as an opportunity to create a new blog post or a short video to answer the question. Just be careful not to fall into the "boring FAQ" type of content. This should be much more personal, informative, and educational. Start creating a resource library you can use whenever another person asks you the same question. This will save you and your staff from having to spend 10-20 minutes answering redundant questions.

3. Showcase Your Clients and Leverage Your Successes

Showcase testimonials, clients, stories, what worked for your clients in the past and how. Chances are there are other potential clients out there with a similar issue who will identify with the stories you share. By showcasing your clients, you'll create a greater affinity with your market.

4. Free Resources

We've talked about this in detail in Chapter 6. It's basically offering your potential clients free resources and helpful information. For example, if you're a website designer and a customer comes in with a very limited (or practically nonexistent) budget, instead of turning them away, discounting your services (and losing money), or spending hours and hours explaining how they can do it on their own, you can create a "How to build a website on your own" blueprint and share it with them. It may seem counterintuitive, but if you're truly in the business to serve people, you'll want to help people. At the very least, it's a great way of not being a jerk and saying, "You're too broke to afford me." Instead, you send them a quick link that helps them out and doesn't cost you anything. I've personally applied this strategy with clients who can't afford us and some have actually come back when they could afford to pay for our services. When they don't, they usually use one of our affiliate links and we've actually made money. For a hosting company, we get $60 as a commission for anyone that signs up. Not bad for a ten minute conversation with one of our team members.

Leveraging Other People's Content

Creating 100% of your content can sometimes become overwhelming. There's a great way to complement your own content and that's with curated content, aka, content from other people. It allows you to keep your social media fresh and keep delivering value. By spending some time bringing your audience the best quality and most relevant content from other people, you will save them time and help you on your path of becoming an authority on the subject.

Many times people want to learn in a short time what took experts years to understand. Sometimes just telling people what to read and who to listen to can save them months of research and wasted time consuming outdated information.

I'm a marketer and I hate email newsletters—like *really* hate them—because most of them are fluffy, useless, a waste of time, and contain no real value, effort, or thought. You can tell I hate newsletters right? Yet one of my favorite emails I get every week is from Peter Diamandis, a futurist, scientist, and entrepreneur.

I've been subscribed to Peter Diamandis's emails and newsletter for a few years now and I never get tired of them, and they're long emails! Why? Because he saves me countless hours of Googling or watching bad Youtube videos trying to find the stuff I'm interested in.

I'm busy running a full time business, but I'm fascinated with where we're going as a species and how technology is accelerating our cultural changes. I'm interested in things like technology, innovation, healthcare, artificial intelligence, extending the human lifespan, how technology is disrupting the way we live and work, going to Mars, and other wacky stuff. Peter's weekly emails help me figure out what to focus on and what to keep an eye out for.

He runs full time companies in a lot of these areas and is surrounded by people who are involved in them. He writes well thought out and insightful articles on his blog and emails a plain text version to his subscribers. I read *every single one of them*.

His team also does a phenomenal job of sending out newsletters that share the top things happening in tech, which contain links to the original content or some obscure esoteric article I would never find on my own. They add a short summary in the email with 1) what it is, and 2) why it's important.

They've done all the work for me. I trust the team because I know they do their research and check their sources, so often I don't click on each article they curated unless it really interests me. I still get a solid grasp of where things are going despite not being involved with them on a daily basis.

With content curation, you're doing the same thing for your audience and creating affinity with them. By simplifying and filtering out information, you're building trust with your people.

How To Build An Audience

We covered these earlier, unintentionally, but I want to make it crystal clear how you can build an audience. In your traffic generation efforts, make sure you're constantly including calls to action and sending people back to your conversion pages. Having a lead that has raised their hand and is interested in taking the journey with you across your Bridge is ultimately our goal. Here are the three ways to build your audience and grow the number of people interested in your brand.

1. Build It From Scratch

This is often the hardest one and takes the longest. You can do this by using organic SEO, reaching out to people on social media directly via a message, following them, liking their accounts, and commenting on their stuff. One shortcut for targeted engagement is to engage the followers of a top brand or person. For example, an accountant or lawyer looking for small business owners can go to the profiles of Quickbooks, Small Business Administration, Chase Small Business, or Square Payments and follow their fans. Chances are their fans are the same demographic as your potential clients.

You could also cold email people, just be careful not to get blacklisted by spamming people. Cold outreach is fine as long as you don't upload a list of 10,000 names to an email service and blast them with an unwanted message.

2. Borrow or Rent It

Media appearances, guest podcasts, guest blogging, and influencer partnerships all fall under this category. All you have to do is ask. They may say no, but one opportunity from an influential person or brand can change the game for you. This is probably the cheapest, best, and fastest way to get highly qualified people into your marketing funnel. Create an affiliate program of your own and incentivize people to promote you.

Renting an audience sort of falls into the next category, but I'm mostly referring to people with their own email lists they've built over time and have explicit permission to communicate with. It can also be social media accounts with large follower accounts. They will often allow you to send one or even multiple communications to their audience for a fee.

3. Pay For It

This falls into the last chapter of the Client Acquisition Blueprint. Simply put, you pay for the attention and the opportunity to build a loyal following. Big companies will spend millions on brandwing campaigns to earn the loyalty of people. Most small businesses can't afford that luxury, so I recommend that if you're looking to pay, find a way to get a return on your investment (ROI) from every dollar you spend. Don't throw money at branding campaigns unless you're ok with not getting an ROI. If your bank takes "likes" as currency, then that's cool too and please refer me to your banker.

The Power Of Positioning

My office is right on the Walk of Fame in Hollywood, just two blocks away from where they host the Oscars every year. If you've ever visited the area or live here, you surely know it's not all glamor and high-class like you see on TV. If you haven't been here, sorry for the spoilers. I've seen Spider-Man smoking weed behind the CVS, homeless people peeing on the floor, and high pressure sales people hustling tourists into a bus for a tour of celebrities' homes.

And yet every year, people still travel from around the world to see the Walk of Fame and lay down on the floor next to the star of their favorite celebrity to take a picture. Why is that? Why do people travel thousands of miles to lay down on dirty pavement? There are dirty pavements to lay down on in literally every city. The answer: positioning. Each tourist attraction is positioned in our society and culture as the place to go to.

This process of building expert status, celebrity, and authority has a profound and long lasting psychological impact on your audience. It's what allows you to go from chasing people to people chasing you. Some might be experts in their field through their degrees and experience, but in the minds of people, they don't have expert positioning and they're just like every other person with degrees and experience. This happens often with doctors, accountants, attorneys, and consultants. They simply lack the proper positioning to stand out.

By creating relevant content to post on your website, blog, social media, and other channels, you can achieve more visibility, connect with other influencers, and participate in the public discourse as an expert. This will help you differentiate from your competitors and generate interest in your business. It creates more opportunities for you and allows you to maximize the efficiency of your efforts. You'll become the go-to expert and the only logical choice in prospects' minds when it comes to solving a specific issue. This is only possible with a well-executed positioning strategy.

There are, of course, many more ways of getting organic attention, such as referrals, viral campaigns, offline methods, and regular word of mouth. In this chapter we focused on the most common ones and those that have been proven to work for the vast majority of businesses and entrepreneurs. Using these methods, we've been able to help clients reach millions of people every month, increase the number of people interested in their services, decrease sales resistance and ultimately increase their overall revenue.

Not everything will work for you, and you need to find your own combination of media, style, channels, and subjects that work best for you and your company. Over time, you'll be able to position yourself as an expert authority in your industry, and eventually manufacture celebrity and influencer status of your own. It should be noted here that by "celebrity" we're not referring to a Hollywood star or a globally known company, but simply a well-known persona in the relevant circles and among the audience you're most interested in serving. Not everyone needs or wants to be a Kanye West.

By creating authority through content and strategically designing your brand positioning, you'll also be increasing your organic traffic. Or, in other words, you'll get "free" organic attention.

Get A **FREE Video Deep-Dive Training** and See Real Examples of Our Top Converting Pages Here: **clientacquisitionblueprint.com/freegift**

Paid Online Advertising

CHAPTER 10

The fuel for consistent and predictable growth.

You can certainly thrive relying solely on organic methods. Companies like Tesla, Costco, Sriracha, and Zara all do well without spending a dime on paid advertising. If you have the proper positioning, whether it's through the methods described earlier or by creating raving fans through your products, you won't have to spend money on advertising.

If you find that the organic strategies do not give you the results you're looking for or you want to grow faster, paid advertising gives you that much needed fuel. Think of paid online advertising as a faucet. You can turn it on or up when you want more water, you can turn it off or down when you want less water.

I personally love a mix of both paid advertising and organic growth strategies. With the right combination, your revenue can skyrocket. Achieving your growth goals is simply a matter of dialing things in and turning them up. You increase your budget a bit on your ads, launch a new campaign, and produce consistent content to get in front of people consistently. You then retarget people who have interacted with your brand to close the loop and get them into your automated funnel. You then test, optimize, test, and optimize again. This system can create amazing results!

But paid advertising can often feel like a gamble. You're putting money in and hoping you'll get more money back in return. Sometimes you'll launch campaigns and they're an instant money maker. Other times you're not so lucky. In advertising, you're often playing the game of 'Who can spend more to acquire this customer?' Your competitors are also buying advertising and some might have deeper pockets. So how do you maximize your returns and avoid loss?

When To Start Advertising

According to the Small Business Administration, as of 2014 there were around 28.2 million small businesses in the US. Of these, over 80% don't have employees and struggle to make a mere $44,000 a year in gross revenue. Naturally at that level, it's tough to spend $10 on advertising.

1. Make money first.

When a new business comes to me and says they need help with their marketing but their revenues are below $100,000, I usually advise them to go knock on doors, cold call, network, and implement the first nine chapters of the Client Acquisition Blueprint to at least get to around $100,000 in sales before thinking of investing in advertising.

If you're one of the 80% of businesses just getting started, just get something up, then go out there and hustle, talk to people, and learn about your clients. You can go online to Vistaprint and get brochures, postcards, and business cards. Go on Squarespace and get a website for a few dollars. Just start and focus on growing your revenue.

2. Put your business systems in place.

You have to really dial in your business before spending money on advertising. You need to have a product or service people want, have an easy way for people to give you money, and have your systems for delivery dialed in.

How are you answering your phone or emails when someone submits an inquiry? Are you winging it every time because 'it's all in your head'? Write it down, put it on a checklist, and make it easy for someone else to follow the same process.

Make sure you have some basic automation and tracking in place to handle the new influx of business. Otherwise you'll get the calls, inquiries, and opportunities, but they'll fall off your desk without you even realizing it.

Even when business owners think they have it all together, I've seen them shut off their successful ad campaigns because they're 'too busy' and can't handle the work. It's a good problem to have but it's almost as bad as the feast and famine, cashflow rollercoaster most businesses find themselves in. I've seen business owners not put the proper tracking in place or write contact information on sticky notes, then toss them out with their lunch leftovers.

3. It takes courage!

Have you ever heard the expression, "It takes money to make money"? I disagree with that statement 90% of the time because you can find ways to make money without having to spend money. But in advertising, that's definitely true.

More importantly, *making money takes courage*. The courage to go out there, learn a new skill, learn how things work, and then just take an informed leap of faith. You never really know if a campaign will work, but you can't get gun shy and start prematurely tweaking campaigns before they get a chance to optimize or produce enough data.

If all that sounds too scary, and it most likely does – nobody wants to spend money without any guarantees or assurances—don't worry. In this chapter, we'll go through the basics of paid advertising, as well as some tips and pointers on how to maximize your advertising efforts.

Legal Disclaimer

Because we're going to be talking about spending money to grow a business, I feel like I should reiterate this. Although you obviously know this is a marketing book, some people might think this is specific advice for their business. It's not. It's a framework I've used when working on marketing campaigns for clients. This book and material is for information and illustrative purposes only and does not purport to show actual results. It is not, and should not be regarded as investment, legal, or professional advice. Results are likely to vary substantially. The platforms and strategies are not guaranteed to achieve profits, losses, or results similar to those discussed. So, with that out of the way, let's continue with our exploration of paid advertising.

How to Not Lose Money

Before you start with your paid advertising campaigns, you need to get a few baseline things in place. Especially if this is your first experience with paid advertising and the basic metrics to track aren't all that clear quite yet.

The best way to think of your first test is that you're paying for data. It's the price of experience and education that comes with running a test. A great way to prevent major losses is to find somebody with experience in your industry and paid advertising to guide you through the process. If they have experience in your industry, they most likely have an idea of what doesn't work and can save you time and money by avoiding unnecessary tests.

Another absolute must for running paid ads is having your dedicated conversion pages in place. Make sure the message is using one of the copywriting formulas we talked about in the Conversion Pages chapter. Don't start by talking about yourself, rather focus on your audience, their problem, and how you can solve it. Have one call to action and make it easy for people to become a lead or customer.

Once you have these in place, the next question is—which platforms to use?

Where Should I Advertise?

Just like with organic growth strategies, there's an array of options. Some options are solid and have been the leaders for years, such as Google Adwords and Facebook Ads. Platforms like Pinterest Ads, LinkedIn Ads and Twitter Ads have a comparatively small user base and are still competing for market share, if you can call it a competition.

In the third quarter of 2016, Fortune Magazine reported that out of the $17.6 billion spent in online advertising, 99% of that was spent on Google and Facebook. Google made up 54% of online ad spending, with Facebook coming in at 45%, and 1% for everyone else. Needless to say, Facebook and Google are the undisputed kings of online advertising.

If you're working with a small budget, I recommend sticking with the mature advertising platforms that have been proven to get results for businesses in your industry. As your budget increases or if you have a discretionary budget, testing other untapped platforms can prove to be lucrative if you can figure out the right medium, market, and message fit.

My personal goal with paid advertising is to create a predictable growth channel so that you can predict revenue month in and month out. Once you have some winning campaigns, you can diversify and make up a unique bouquet of platforms that work for your business.

One of the appeals of paid online advertising is that it can be much more cost effective than traditional media, especially as your ad spend increases. According to the American Marketing Association, in 2017 during the NFL Super Bowl, the cost of a 30 second commercial was around $5 million USD. This was to reach around 111 million people. When determining ad spend, large companies tend to consider cost per thousand impressions, expressed as CPM (the M stands for 1,000 or 'mille').

The CPM for the Super Bowl in 2017 was $45. Compare that to the average CPM on Facebook in Q3 of 2016 which was between $7.19 and $7.34, according to AdEspresso's analysis of over $100M in ad spend for the same quarter. The difference is night and day.

Of course, most of us aren't buying super expensive TV spots like this, but even on a smaller scale and even if the costs were equal, online advertising gives you much more control, tools, and data than offline advertising.

For the price and time it takes to produce just one TV ad, you can have several paid online campaigns running on different platforms. And the best part – they will most likely be much more effective in providing you an ROI.

How Online Advertising Works: A Quick Look at Online Advertising Platforms

Both Google and Facebook have self serve platforms that allow you to go in and create your own ads. You can literally launch a new ad in five to ten minutes! They might not be good ads, but the technology is there that allows you to do so.

As with all marketing, understanding who to target, what to say, and how to create effective campaigns is a whole different conversation which we've covered in the previous chapters of your Client Acquisition Blueprint. Having someone to walk you through is always my suggestion.

If you can't afford to hire someone or you have an in-house team member handling your advertising, Facebook and Google both have amazing help centers and video tutorials to walk you step by step through how to create your campaigns. They want to make it easy for you to spend money with them and they actually want to help you create profitable campaigns. If you're making a profit, you're more likely to pay them more money to advertise.

The most common approach to paid advertising is to set up a **Search Campaign** or **PPC (pay per click) campaigns** on any of the major search networks: Google, Yahoo or Bing. This is where your ad appears only when people search for your product or service. These ads might also appear on map and navigation applications on mobile.

You choose the most relevant keywords and set a budget for how much you're willing to pay to get a click. These keywords should be the same as or very similar to the ones your potential clients would use to search for your product or service. A dentist in Houston might chose keywords like 'cosmetic dentist,' 'braces,' or 'tooth pain,' then set her location settings to cover a 25 mile radius from Houston.

The other option on search engines is display advertising, which is the type of online advertising that resembles an ad you'd see on a billboard or bus stop. They're the ads that have attractive banners and images. It displays ads across various websites relevant to your business, such as news sites, blogs, online shops, etc.

The option outside of search advertising is social media advertising. This differs from organic social media marketing in that you're paying to show your posts to completely new people who haven't necessarily engaged with your brand.

With organic social media marketing, the things you post are only shown to people who already like or follow your page (aka have engaged with your brand). If those people share your post, then their network sees it. Viral organic campaigns can have a huge network effect but they're extremely difficult to strategically and predictably recreate. This limits your ability to grow and reach new people.

That's the void that social media advertising fills. There are advertising options on Facebook, Twitter, and LinkedIn, among others, that offer to set up highly focused campaigns to target a very specific audience.

Simply stated, you pay a company like Facebook and they show your ads to more people. The beauty of a platform like Facebook, and the reason why they dominate the space, is that the level of targeting and data that they give you access to is unprecedented.

Facebook is the largest database of humans ever, and they know more information about people than you might realize. You can target a 42 year old conservative male in Pleasanton, Nebraska who owns a Ford, is a baseball fan, and enjoys Budweiser. Or you can target a 28 year old in Silicon Valley who has an income above $75,000 a year and has a birthday in March. Though these are silly examples and I haven't tried targeting to that level, they are possible inside of Facebook's Ad Manager.

These types of online advertising can each work on their own, or you can choose to create your own personalized mix. Either way, the fact that you can obtain very detailed performance reports on each of these gives you the liberty to react in time and find a better solution if you find that your initial idea isn't working. If things do work, you can quickly scale.

Most Popular Platforms

We touched on most of the ad platforms available, but to get you started, here's a short list of the most popular platforms you can choose from.

> **LEARN MORE NOW—CLAIM YOUR FREE GIFT!**
>
> In our *Client Acquisition Blueprint Masterclass*, we walk you step-by-step through **how to set up successful ads** and how to avoid unnecessary testing, *plus* show you examples of our best campaigns.
>
> If you want to learn more, just claim your *FREE* **Gift** here: **clientacquisitionblueprint.com/freegift** ($297 Value, Yours *FREE*)

1. Google AdWords

Since spring of 2011, there were over 1.2 million businesses using Google's paid advertising and Google also takes 97% of mobile search spend. You can find the resources on setting up your first campaign at https://adwords.google.com/home/resources/.

2. Facebook Ads

Even if you think your audience is not on Facebook, the fact is they are. From doctors, lawyers, busy business owners, stay at home moms, and decision makers of major corporations, Facebook has a vast user base. With nearly 2 billion users who connect on a daily basis, it's suitable for nearly all industries. A short video or a simple ad can have a major impact on your website traffic, your lead flow, and your bottom line. You can find more resources on getting started with Facebook ads at: https://www.facebook.com/business/resources.

3. Industry Websites

We mentioned these in Chapter 4 as a must-have for online presence. But, what's more, many offer advertising space that you can use to complement your paid campaign. For real estate agents, Zillow and Trulia both offer advertising. Same goes for healthcare, attorneys, and just about every major industry.

4. Other Search Engines

1. YouTube: Owned by Google and managed through your Google Adwords dashboard.

2. Bing, Yahoo, YP.com: These are still popular search engines, though it's not really fair to compare them to Google in terms of daily traffic.

3. Yelp: It's a great tool for local traffic, organic traffic, and reputation building. They also offer paid advertising. This can be especially beneficial for new businesses looking to get an initial boost in traffic.

5. Other Social Platforms

Instagram is owned by Facebook and you can manage your ads in the Facebook Ads Manager. LinkedIn, Twitter, Snapchat, Pinterest, and nearly all social media now has the option to advertise in addition to their organic tools.

If you're not quite sure where to begin, take a look at other companies your clients buy from, or look at the top five companies in your industry (not your competitors), and analyze how they get their traffic. There's no shame in learning from those who already know the game and spend millions to acquire customers! There are actually great tools to do so, like https://www.spyfu.com/ and https://www.semrush.co, to name two.

How Much Should I Spend?

If you recall from the Strategy chapter, we talked about how to create a marketing budget. Most of our clients find a way to spend 10-20% of their top line revenue in marketing. To start, half of their budget might go towards execution and team, either by hiring an in-house marketing team or paying an agency partner. The other half of their budget would go directly to advertising spend.

Let's take a very simple example of a small law firm aiming to make $600,000 in revenue for the year in new cases. 10%, or $60,000, is the set marketing budget, out of which $30,000 is allocated for staff salaries or agency fees. The remaining $30,000 is allocated to be spent on advertising over the course of 12 months. That's a budget of $2,500 per month in advertising spend.

Once you know how much you're willing to spend a month, you can set a daily budget and then make weekly adjustments, increasing or decreasing your daily spend to stay within the monthly budget. If your campaign is profitable, then you might choose to increase the budget.

For a small business looking to get started with around $1000, a good number to consider is anything between $15 and $30 a day and then scale up from there. Meaning that your initial monthly budget would be somewhere between $500 and $1000, which you can then increase.

How Much Does It Cost?

There are three main ways you can get billed, each of them varying slightly depending on the platform. Each charge type is platform specific so you're best off reading their terms of service to see which billing type is best for your goals. When you create your ads, you'll usually select your preferred method.

1. **Clicks**. The number of people who clicked on your ad. Common with Google Adwords.

2. **Impressions**. The number of people (usually expressed in thousands) that were exposed to your ad, regardless of whether they clicked on it or not. This is common on YouTube and Facebook.

3. **Conversions**. The number of people turned from visitors to leads by sharing their contact information with you. This can be common on industry websites where they only charge you per lead. Facebook allows

you to optimize for lead conversion instead of just impressions and they'll show your ad to people who are more likely to convert into leads.

You can get more detailed than this, but clicks and impressions are the two most common ways of getting charged.

In terms of costs, this is one where it really depends. It depends on the platform, location, your industry, your ad, the messaging, and current market trends. For Google Adwords, some industries see clicks of only a few dollars, while other industries like banks, law, automotive, and real estate see clicks of around $20, $40, and above.

According to AdEspresso's same study of 2016, the average cost per click on Facebook was $0.27. We've gotten website clicks for some industries as low as $0.10, whereas for others we've spent around $5 a click because of the type of people we were targeting.

At the end of the day, we're after a return on our investment, not the lowest costs. Some of our clients have been ok with paying as high as $60 per click on Google Adwords because we know our conversion rates, our client value, and we know that even at such a high cost, we have the opportunity to make a lot more in revenue. If we can put $1,000 in advertising and get $3,000 in sales, then things starts to make sense and we can start creating that predictable revenue every business needs to thrive.

The Profit Path Part II

In the Strategy chapter we mentioned the Profit Path, or, simply put, the basic math that answers the question, "How am I going to make money?" This same principle is even more important now that we're spending money on advertising.

Profitable advertising campaigns are our goal, so let's take a look at a better question than, "How much does it cost?" and look at how you can actually make money with advertising.

Google Adwords	SPEND	VISITS	LEADS	CLIENTS	REVENUE
EXAMPLE	$1,500	50	5	1	$5,000
CASE STUDY	$1,945.54	56	25	3	**$21,500**

Let's take the earlier example of the law firm and say the firm's average client is worth $5,000 in attorney fees. They decide to run a campaign on Google AdWords and they have a $1,500 advertising budget per month allocated for the campaign. They're a bit hesitant and nervous about spending money since it's their first time advertising and they're not sure this campaign will work for them.

Their competition is relatively high and their cost per click (or CPC) for that specific group of keywords is an average of $30. This would get him 50 clicks or visits to his website. With a 10% lead conversion, he'll get five leads (either phone calls or form submissions), and if 20% of these leads turn into paying clients, he closes one new client at $5,000.

So, looking at it from this perspective, the $1,500 per month that might have looked scary the first time around doesn't seem to be quite as intimidating anymore.

If we calculate the Return on Investment (ROI) for this campaign (revenue earned divided by ad spend), we can see that every month he has a 333% return on investment, or roughly a ratio of 3:1. In other words, the ad campaign returns $3 for every $1 he puts in. We've actually ran this exact campaign for tax law firms and have gotten these results, often better.

Using Facebook Ads, the same framework applies. For our consulting client, Michael Rozbruch, we use Facebook to target accountants who might be interested in doing IRS representation work but who also might be afraid of doing the work. Instead of advertising for them to buy our expensive training program directly, we invite them to download a free report first, then we continue to deliver value to them via email.

We know that once they're in our ecosystem, we can make them relevant sales offers. This campaign has resulted in over 1,800 leads, 200 of which have bought one training product or another ranging from $50 to $2,000. After looking at our data, we realized a few of his higher level consulting clients who have paid him $18,000+ initially came in from this free three page PDF we promoted on Facebook. That's the power all the elements in the Client Acquisition Blueprint have when deployed together!

Once you have a formula and understand a market, you can dial things in and make decisions on when to increase your spend and where.

For your business, you can just change the values in the formula and test to find what works for you. If you find your profit margins can't support a 3 to 1 return on ad spend up front, then you need to look at what the lifetime value of your client is. How can you add more value later in the journey and make more money? How can you get referrals and grow organically now that you have a client? If you're making some money and acquiring clients, then you have an opportunity, you just have to keep working at it and implementing the Client Acquisition Blueprint.

That's where the Profit Path helps clarify things for you. Here's how to structure your own Profit Path and the key metrics to track so you can create your own winning campaigns:

1. **Average Client Value**: Look at your last 12 months of transactions and determine what your average client is worth to you.
    a. **On a single transaction**: How much do they spend with you their first time around? Caution: this is where most business owners stop and they

        leave money on the table for their competitors to snatch up.

    b.   **Client Lifetime Value**: How long does each client stay with you and continue to buy your products or services? Refer back to the value ladder concept in Chapter 1 to increase your client's lifetime value. I usually start by simply figuring out my clients' 12 month value. How much do they spend with us during the first 12 months?

2.   Set your **Advertising Budget**.

3.   **Website Metrics**:

    a.   Traffic: How many visits do you need to your website?

    b.   Conversion Rate: What percentage of your visitors take action and become a lead? I call this your Lead Conversion Rate.

4.   **Sales Metrics**: How many people do you need to talk to in order to get a sale? I call this your Sales Conversion Rate.

5.   **Costs and Returns**: Is this campaign profitable?

    a.   **Cost Per Lead (CPL)**: How much did it cost you to acquire a lead? Divide the ad spend by the number of leads generated by your campaign to find your CPL.

    b.   **Cost Per Acquisition (CPA)**: How much did it cost you to acquire a client? Divide the ad spend by the number of clients you got from your campaign to find your CPA.

    c.   **Return on Investment**: Revenue earned divided by ad spend.

A quick note on calculations

I usually make two sets of calculations depending on what information I'm looking for. If I'm looking to evaluate just my advertising campaigns themselves, then I leave out any money paid to manage the campaigns, such as money paid to my team or agency partner. I calculate cost per lead, cost per acquisition, and ROI by only factoring in the money paid directly to advertisers. This allows me to measure the effectiveness of ad specific factors such as ad type, targeting, creative (message, design, media type), the ad platform itself, and optimization methods used.

If I'm looking to evaluate a specific team member or agency, I'd take a longer date range, say six months, and factor their salary or payment. This way, my metrics for making decisions are clear. If I'm evaluating just my advertising and not the person managing the ads, then I'd make those calculations on a more consistent basis, at least weekly or monthly.

It's important to know these numbers during the life of your advertising campaign, but you should also structure your Profit Path from the beginning so you're clear on what to track. Set baseline targets, even if in the beginning you're just taking educated guesses.

How to Maximize Your Advertising Efforts

Advertising can be pretty simple. It's a pay-to-play game that with some planning and strategic actions can have a very strong and positive impact on your growth. Once you find your own magic formula that works, keep doing it until it stops working.

When your magic formula stops working, it's perfectly fine to pause, take a step back, and search for what to improve. I recommend launching campaigns on a regular schedule so you don't lose momentum. While your initial campaigns are still working, start testing new campaigns until you find new winners.

Here's a simple list of questions to ask before launching new ads and when you want to optimize existing ads.

1. **The Ad Creative**: What your ad says and what it looks like.
   a. Headline: Does it call out the prospect and draw them in?

    b.   Is your message direct and succinct? Is it compelling and remarkable?

    c.   Is the image or video relevant? Have you tried less text, more text, different colors? If it's a static image, would it make sense to make a short video?

    d.   Is the call to action clear? What do you want them to do?

2. **The Ad Targeting**: Who you're showing your ad to.

    a.   Is your targeting on point or is it too broad and your ad is being shown to people with no interest in what you have to offer?

    b.   Does the messaging match the specific audience or are you grouping everyone together?

3. **Conversion Pages**

    a.   Does the messaging match your advertisement?

    b.   Is your call to action above the fold (viewable without the user having to scroll)?

    c.   How well does the conversion page appear on mobile devices?

    d.   How can the design be improved? Are there non essential elements that might be hurting your conversion?

    e.   Is your offer relevant and attractive?

4. **Sales Conversion**

    a.   Do you have the proper automation in place?

    b.   What can you further improve in your communication to make the potential clients' experience even more pleasant and enjoyable?

    c.   What script do you follow when you speak with your potential customers on the phone? Is it being followed consistently?

    d.   How easy is it to give you money? Are there long delays in your sales process?

Every time you launch a campaign, you should absolutely run at least two versions of everything. That way you can see what works better and improve only the things that are working. Cut the things that don't work or try a variation. This is called a split test. At the very minimum, you need to be split testing your conversion pages, your ads, and your targeting.

Choose Carefully Who to Target

There are two final concepts in advertising that are absolutely essential. One is targeting, which we've covered briefly, and the other retargeting.

Targeting is exactly what the name implies. Look back at your Perfect Client Profile and use this to target your ideal clients online. All of the major platforms give their advertisers the ability to choose exactly who should see a specific ad.

Each platform gives you different tools, and some options that may be available on Facebook might not be available on Google Adwords, and vice versa. The combinations can be endless, but some of the targeting options to consider are:

▷ Keywords (on Google) or Interests (on Facebook)
▷ Age + Gender
▷ Marital/Relationship Status
▷ Education
▷ Occupation
▷ Location
▷ Income

So, if you want to get more foot traffic to your organic juicing business, you might create a set of Google ads that appear on search and the mobile app. The people you want to reach live mainly in Los Angeles, are between 24-35 and are interested in cold press juices, so you set your targeting to only a ten mile radius and select the relevant keywords.

You might also run a Facebook ad targeting only women interested in the major organic food brands who are within a 50 mile radius and have a household income of more than $75,000. The call to action on Adwords would be to come into the store, while the offer on Facebook might be to sign up for a subscription box of monthly juices.

One of the ways we've been able to reduce ad costs and increase our clients' revenue is through strategically choosing segments of a market to target. An insurance broker client came to us for marketing help. He wanted to advertise, but the problem was that the competition for his products was fierce. An insurance broker has access to countless policies, but if they're trying to sell car insurance to everyone, they're competing with companies who have hundreds of millions to throw at advertising. In this case, it drove the cost of advertising on Google to an astronomical level. Since each car insurance policy is not as profitable, he'd lose money if he tried to play that game.

Instead, we decided to narrow our focus to commercial truck insurance. These policies were worth thousands in commissions to the client, compared to the hundreds (at best) that a regular car insurance policy would bring in. The best part: large companies showed very little interest in focusing on a niche market like that and they left the playing field wide open. Our ad costs were reasonable and the payoff was a lot higher. We had to hire dedicated staff, change the way he answered his phones, and eventually rebrand and restructure his entire company to serve that market.

My wife is an interior architect and designer, and after a few attempts at growing a traditional firm doing residential and commercial projects, she decided to narrow her focus even further by specializing in medical interior design. Since large design firms only have a subpage on their website dedicated to healthcare design and show little interest in launching a serious campaign, it also leaves the field wide open. Her firm, LA Healthcare Design, is now one of the top rated medical interior architecture, design, and construction firms in the country.

In the strategy chapter, we covered how to make these strategic decisions through identifying the most profitable services and the type of clients that allow you to do your best work. Some of these decisions might cause your entire business to shift and focus on that target market. Other times, it's simply a way to create additional profit centers in your business through strategic advertising and marketing campaigns that complement what you're currently doing.

Retargeting—Closing The Loop In Your Traffic Strategies

When you get into paid advertising, you're really playing the game of, "How much am I willing to spend to acquire a client?" That can be a dangerous game because there's always someone who has a higher risk tolerance than you and willing to spend more.

With paid advertising, you're paying for the attention of new people who haven't seen your brand, and for people who have seen your brand but haven't bought. That's where retargeting comes in.

Have you ever searched for something on Amazon and didn't buy it, but all of the sudden you started seeing their ads everywhere? They track the pages you've viewed, then show you an ad because you're more likely to buy since you've already indicated you were interested. The ads are highly relevant and more effective, and can have enormous effects on your revenue because they recapture potential sales.

Practical applications for businesses outside of ecommerce are the following:

1. A person was exposed to your ad for a lead magnet and clicked on it, but didn't convert from visitor to lead. Retargeting will expose this same person to the same ad again with the purpose of achieving the conversion.

2. Someone searches for your business, goes to your website,

but leaves without taking any action. You can retarget them to contact you via a dedicated contact page.

3. Someone visits your law firm's blog and reads an article on estate planning. You then retarget them to a retirement planning lead magnet.

4. If someone watches your video all the way through, they're now highly familiar with you and are no longer a new audience. They're much more likely to engage with subsequent content and offers.

Retargeting is especially good because it lowers your ad spend substantially, it decreases your cost per acquisition (CPA) and cost per lead (CPL), and it also closes the loop on your marketing effort.

Recap—What to Measure?

An ad campaign is only as effective as the metrics you track. If you don't track your numbers, you'll be making decisions in the dark. You might think your ads suck, when in reality they're getting you solid results and just need a little boost in order to get faster results. Conversely, you might get super busy all of the sudden and think it's your ad campaigns when in reality, it's from organic search and you're simply not attributing the lead source properly. Consistently looking at your ad campaigns and knowing what key metrics to track is a must for profitable advertising. Here's a quick recap list of the key metrics:

▷ Ad spend
▷ Visits
▷ Leads
▷ Landing Page Conversion %
▷ Clients
▷ Sales Conversion %: Out of the leads, how many converted to clients? In 30 days? 90 days? 180 days? 12 months?

▷ Revenue
▷ Cost per Lead
▷ Cost per Acquisition
▷ Return on Investment
▷ Client Lifetime Value

How to use these metrics

If the visitors are not converting into leads, then the issue might be landing page related. On the other hand, if leads are not converting into clients, then the issue is most likely related to your sales process.

My goal is to give you the tools to be able to assess the effectiveness of your campaigns. You can gather a lot more data and get really granular, but these can serve as a distraction from the bigger picture and running your business.

When you fully commit to paid advertising and find a few winning campaigns, that's all you might need. Ultimately these two chapters, organic and paid growth, are the keys to fuel your dreams, and they give you options.

Your ability to get attention for your business is the reason you'll have the opportunity to serve more people. When you have the full Client Acquisition Blueprint in place and are consistently getting attention, you'll be able to create predictable cash flow and acquire clients month in and month out. With a steady flow of clients, you'll be able to grow your business, hire new staff, invest back into your business, and avoid those stressful days at the end of the month when you don't know how you're going to survive.

BUILDING AN EPIC BUSINESS

We've made it to the end of the book! In it, we went through the ten principal things that will help you grow your business and build a sustainable marketing strategy. Some things you might have already known, but I encourage you to really ask yourself, "Does my bank account and my business success prove that I already know them?" Knowledge and ideas in business are worthless without execution.

Early on in my business I went in to see a potential client, a CEO of a multimillion dollar business. He was in his 60s, vastly more successful than anyone I had met at the time, and three times my age. I was nervous, thinking to myself, "What can I possibly teach to this guy? He's already successful and I have no idea how to help him." Nonetheless, I went to the meeting thinking that the worst that could happen is I would be out of there in five minutes and go get some Chipotle. I was also curious to see what someone at that level needed, because he had called me from a referral and was interested in learning about what we did.

I entered his office trembling, but still managing to hold myself together. I started asking questions about his business and what he wanted, then pulled my Macbook out of my bag and began showing him a few campaigns we were running. He sat there for an hour, listening to me, asking detailed questions, asking me to dive deeper into some of the advertising campaigns, and writing down notes.

What amazed me is that he was actually listening and actively learning, despite the fact that he had more experience in marketing than I did. He spent more money in one month of marketing than I had made in my entire lifetime, and probably more than my top clients at the time made in an entire year. The lesson I learned: always be learning. When you think you know everything is usually when you stop searching for answers and stop improving. If you stop improving, you'll eventually stop growing.

Unfortunately, I didn't get a chance to go to Chipotle that day because the meeting ran late and I had another meeting afterwards. Fortunately, I got a new client for Just Digital and we were able to crush it for that company.

The Ten Steps To An Epic Marketing Strategy and Online Presence

A solid **strategy** is the center and base of every marketing effort in your business. What do we really want, where are we going, and why, are all questions to be answered in your strategy.

Next is your **brand identity**: the message, logo, colors, photography, and every visual aspect of your brand. These will be clearly transmitted through your **website**, **online profiles**, and **social media**. The foundation is set, and your business is on the map.

Conversion and automation help bridge the gap between attention and revenue. With **irresistible offers** and **lead magnets** strategically placed on your **conversion pages**, you'll be able to convert viewers into leads and attention into profit. However, to be as effective as possible and keep your sanity while running your business, you need to put the proper **automation** into place. This will ensure your business runs smoothly, you deliver massive value, and it serves as the backbone for scaling your business.

However, none of these will do anything without getting massive attention for your business with **organic and paid acquisition strategies**. Producing high quality content consistently and being seen as an **authority** in your industry are the foundation for organic attention. To speed up the process and get predictable revenue growth, **paid advertising** should be implemented.

Everything I've shared in the book are the building blocks I've personally used in building Just Digital and in helping our clients' businesses. There's a lot of information on marketing and it can be overwhelming when trying to decide what to implement. But when you break it down, there are only three areas of focus:

It's not as complex as it might seem at the beginning, and depending on what stage your business is at, you can choose to focus on one area more than the other. Businesses, much like living beings, evolve and need to adapt. At any given moment, you're going to be working on one of these three areas.

THE 3 BUILDING BLOCKS OF MARKETING

1. Unshakeable Foundation
2. Converting Leads to Clients
3. Getting Massive Attention

You got into business to do something you love—***do it on your own terms and live a better life***. So your duty, responsibility, and obligation is to market your business so that you can live out your dreams and create an epic life.

I believe the role of a business is to create value, and you, as the brain, heart, and soul of your business, need to stay true to your central role as *The Value Creator*. Your ability to create value, communicate, and exchange it will determine your success. The Client Acquisition Blueprint aims at helping you grasp the basic marketing principles and *helping you build an epic business so you can live an epic life!*

Work With

 JUST DIGITAL

"Caring about your business as if it were their own, they take the time to help you discover exactly what you want your business to be and where you want it to go, with pinpoint accuracy." Zachary Weil, Executive Producer and Founder of Contact Light Films

Just Digital Inc is a top rated digital marketing agency in Los Angeles. We work with businesses to implement effective marketing campaigns and create epic content. From strategy to execution we consider ourselves partners for all our clients.

With a focus on ROI, we offer web design, graphic design, content creation, social media management, marketing automation, and paid advertising on Google and Facebook. If you'd like to work together, please visit **justdigitalinc.com/apply** or email us at **success@ justdigitalinc.com**

"In less than one month, I have closed enough business to pay for all of the website and lead magnet landing page design and, in addition, the revenue to support many months of AdWords fees." -Greg, CPA

"[They] created a Landing page for my company that's funneling hundreds of leads per month." -David Benitez, Insurance Broker in Los Angeles CA

Acknowledgements
and
Eternal Gratitude

I thought writing a book would be a solitary effort. I imagined myself working alone on my laptop, in some remote cabin for a few weeks, and returning with the 10 marketing commandments. That's far from the truth.

I am extremely blessed to be surrounded by amazing people who believe in our vision to help passionate people succeed. I'm blessed to have met people on my journey that inspired me, mentored me, and believed in me when at times I didn't.

The Just Digital Team

Thanks to my global team at Just Digital for doing an exceptional job with our clients, for being the best in the world at what you do, and for inspiring me to be a better leader. I'm blessed to learn and grow together.

Thanks to my lead team members who kept the ship running while I worked on this project. Your commitment to Just Digital will help tens of thousands of small business owners.

Laurice—You're the #1 graphic / web designer in the world (in my humble opinion). Seriously, you stun me with every design.

Era—You're insanely talented and consistent, that's why you're the best developer in the world. There's nothing you can't figure out. Also, you can stop calling me "Sir", it makes me feel old.

Isaac—Dude, Orlando steaks! That's definitely going to be our thing. Thanks for diving in with both feet. You got a super bright future and I'm eternally grateful for your contributions. #NoSleep #2HoursMax

The "CAB" Team

Thank you to **Alejandra Solis** from Guadalajara, Jalisco, Mexico for managing the project and helping me stay on track. Sorry, we missed the deadline by 4 months, but we made it!

Thanks **Neza** from Athens, Greece for your assistance in making the Client Acquisition Blueprint into what it is today. Without you, this would still be fragmented thoughts and ideas in my Google Drive.

To My Mentors:

Coach Robert, from RSC Business Group in West LA, thank you for our weekly conversations. You help me get out of my head and take action. Thanks for never doubting my dreams or putting them down. You've taught me I can truly do everything I want, but I can't do it all at once. You always have a word of encouragement, wisdom, and practical guidance.

Peter Voogd, Thank you for constantly pushing me to focus on results. I've come a long way since the Lakewood days thanks to you! Selling Cutco when I was 17 was one of the best experiences of my life. Thanks for believing in me and pushing me towards excellence. I could write a book about our journey together! "From the tire to the top"

Harry Redinger, Serendipity is a beautiful thing. Thank you for the opportunity to share this message with your UCLA students.

Our Clients:

We've tested different parts of this simple marketing process with hundreds of clients. To each and every one of you, thank you for entrusting me with your business. I don't take that privilege lightly. I've learned more from you than you can imagine.

To a few clients in particular, aside from having done

awesome stuff together, a personal thank you:

Michael & Roslyn Rozbruch for being genuine and humble people. I absolutely love working together. We continue to strive for more and despite our massive successes, there's never any ego involved.

Hal Elrod, you don't know this but the biggest thing I've learned form you is to *treat people well* and *be extremely grateful for every moment*. Whenever we do something for The Miracle Morning brand, your responses make my day. You always respond with "you're awesome!" or something cheerful. Sending you lots of great healing energy. Kick cancer's a**!

Kevin Ward, a lot has changed since we worked together, but the impact you had on my life and business was bigger than you'll ever know. You inspired me to believe in my dreams. Thanks for the tickets to Brendons event! They changed my life.

The Gurus:

From the marketing world, thanks to Ryan Deiss and Russell Brunson for running world class companies and your unique contributions to digital marketing.

Grant Cardone, You're insane, but it's awesome! Whenever I've felt like quitting, started making excuses, or was feeling sorry for myself, your audio programs and books woke me back up. You've helped me sell a lot of stuff to a lot of people and their lives are better because of it. #BeObsessedOrBeAverage #10x

Brendon Burchard, "I'm here!" Your teachings always balance me out (especially after I listen to Grant Cardone). Your energy brought my wife and I together at High Performance Academy and we've been back to that event every year. You taught me to "bring the joy" to everything I do. The people I've met through you are the most heart centered and beautiful people in the world. You helped clarify my path and made this book happen. At Experts Academy, while you were teaching, I was creating. "The power plant doesn't have energy, it creates it."

I could name every author whose work has inspired me, but that would be a lot of names. To all the "experts", thank you.

My Family:

Mother, Thank you for instilling in me the work ethic and desire for a better life. Nunca tomaré en poco todo el esfuerzo que puso para crearme. Nunca me negó su amor y siempre me apoyó.

Father, Thank you for your relentless dedication to our family. Despite not being my biological father, you are an incredible human being to my mom and I. Gracias por ser el mejor padre del mundo. Gracias por instruirme en el buen camino y por ser la inspiración más grande en mi vida. Gracias por enseñarme a pintar casas, a echarle ganas, y por su amor de padre. Prometo traducir este libro a español para poder ayudar a más gente.

My 3 little sisters, I hope I didn't steer you too far in the wrong direction! Thank you for being amazing sisters. I'm a better person because I baby sat you. You're welcome.

Unnamed Heroes, to the countless friends whom I've met along the way, thank you.

To my wife—My Princess, Queen, Best Friend, and Azizam: At the risk of making this a love letter, I must say you make everything worth it. Every moment we share is magical. This journey with you is beyond extraordinary. I'm still amazed that we run multiple, entirely different companies. Thank you for being my trusted advisor, my biggest cheerleader, and for never letting me settle. Reality is turning out to be way better than I had ever imagined.

About The Author
Hugo Fernandez

Hugo Fernandez is the Founder and CEO of Just Digital Inc, a top rated digital marketing agency based in Los Angeles, serving clients globally.

Hugo has personally helped hundreds of entrepreneurs grow their businesses. He teaches doctors, lawyers, accountants, business owners and freelancers the secrets to attracting a flood of high paying clients, increasing revenues and creating sustainable marketing campaigns.

An entrepreneur by default, his first customer acquisition strategy was to grab customers by the hand at the age of 3, and take them to his mother's food stand in Mexico.

He explains: "I grew up selling tamales door to door in apartment complexes, Mexican candy outside our church, and doing anything I could to make a little extra cash so my parents could afford to put food on the table. All I knew was the hustle. I didn't know it then, but being an entrepreneur was my default and my only way out.

It was a way to survive and it was our shot at having something more. Looking back, this taught me the basics of business and money."

Over the past 10 years he's personally started 10+ brands and businesses. "Some made money, some are still up and running, and others are in the landfill of awesome ideas poorly executed" he says.

Since 2012, he's worked with hundreds of entrepreneurs making their ideas a reality, helping to better market their businesses, get more customers, and increase sales. He's consulted multi-million dollar businesses, high growth startups and new ambitious entrepreneurs.

To connect with Hugo, visit:
https://hugofernandez.com/